The Chosen One...
AUSHIM KHETARPAL

(PRESS REACTIONS)

Businessman leaves everything for Divine search
The Times of India, 2004

Reality in faith
Deccan Cronicle

Match Fixing on Silver Screen Sports promoter to Spiritual Leader
The Hindu

Book and Film on Aushim Khetarpal's life on Silver Screen
Hindustan Times

THE CHOSEN ONE...
AUSHIM KHETARPAL
Believed in only the strength of God

Kanu Priya

Sterling Publishers (P) Ltd.
A-59, Okhla Industrial Area, Phase-II, New Delhi-110020.
Tel: 26387070, 26386209; Fax: 91-11-26383788
E-mail: mail@sterlingpublishers.com
www.sterlingpublishers.com

The Chosen One... Aushim Khetarpal
© 2013, Copyright SSBF
ISBN 978 81 207 8337 9 (PB)
         978 81 207 8336 2 (HB)

All rights are reserved.
No part of this publication may be reproduced, stored in a retrieval system or transmitted, in any form or by any means, mechanical, photocopying, recording or otherwise, without prior written permission of the author.

Printed in India

Printed and Published by Sterling Publishers Pvt. Ltd., New Delhi-110 020.

Preface

I still remember the day when I met Aushim for the first time. It was 27th May 2008. I was at Zee studios, and we were supposed to start recording a programme, "SAI KI MAHIMA". By this time I had been introduced to concepts of soul, spirituality and GOD through discourses like Awakening with Brahma Kumaris. So when I met him, my first thoughts were, 'He is a Page-3 celebrity. What'll he do with SAI BABA?' Then we started talking and he told me about what the programme was. It was a chat show which will be live and people can ask their questions live, which he will answer through Saisatcharitra. I had not heard about it. Believing in Baba and talking about his miracles was something else but this was completely hypothetical. I believed in astrology as I considered it to be a science. I had experimented with it and had seen the results. But answering from Sai Satcharitra was beyond my comprehension and I was quite susceptible. But then the programme started and I saw miracles happening. In every live show, Aushim would just give the answer which looked arbitrary at that time but after few days people would call back that things that he predicted has actually happened. I was amazed to find that almost 90% of the time the answers were true. I was surprised. More than the answers I was intrigued by the person, Aushim. He was not at all the kind of person I had envisaged. Instead, he was quiet opposite. Although, outwardly, he'll come across as a man on a mission, arrogant to few and at times pompous to many; but while doing these shows daily, spending time with him and talking to him, I realized that he has created an outer shield around himself. Deep down he was a simple, gentle and a committed man, carrying too much of a backlog of life's incidences and was in deep pain. He was living his life like a duty, yet he was deeply connected to Baba. His complete faith in Baba and the conviction that his life will change and he'll get back to his glorious years was very endearing. I was curious, as I am the sort of person who loves to unravel mysteries, and this man's life was really a mystery. For me, this was a divine mystery. I could also feel he had a gift of clairvoyance but naively wasn't much aware of it. He connected it to Sai Baba's blessings and always maintained that it was Baba who was answering and he was just the medium.

Aushim always had two kind of people around him, one who had immense faith in his calibre, be it as an entrepreneur, sports promoter, marketing man or Divine healer and others who always had doubts about him. But both the group had reverence and hatred or jealously simultaneously towards him.

Over the years he also had become more of a reactionary, but in last five years what I observed about him was his power to change himself. He is like a chameleon who can change in an instant, which could have been taken as a negative point.

But, soon I realized that this man was on the path of healing and divine truth and this particular trait helps him a lot in his journey.

As I was someone who didn't belong to any of the category I could see his life as a detached observer. In doing so I realized that people around him hardly knew him in the real sense. Two years ago, when he started thinking of making 'Om Allah', a feature film on his life, I felt the script was not right because it was not the true depiction of his life. Aushim is not a healer by choice but I feel he was given the task. Baba revealed Himself to Aushim and then he chose to walk on this path, which is not an easy task if it is not your first choice. But one thing I am sure about him is that once he decides on something, like a true Taurian, he'll take it to the end.

It can be anything -- sports, films, constructing Sai Dham temple or even Self Actualization, he just have to decide, rest he makes it happen.

Before I leave this book in your hands, let me be very honest. I am not a writer; I am a narrator and that also a straight one. So my writing is also like that. I have tried to be as neutral as possible and present the facts in their true sense but I may have erred at some places. As a TV personality, I have been lucky to always receive tremendous love and blessings from all of you. I have survived only because of those blessings, and with my first book, selfishly and shamelessly I request for the same acceptance; but yes, I would also wait for your criticism and suggestions. So, finally I present 'The Chosen One' in your hands for your judgement.

Acknowledgements

I learned a very valuable lesson in last five years of my spiritual journey and that is the value of gratitude and thanks; so, I start my list with my deepest gratitude to Shiv Baba- the Almighty whose existence and presence made me realize the true identity of me and everyone else. Through Shiv Baba, I met Sai Baba, a being who, I feel is the true manifestation of universal love and healing.

HIS constant love and faith in me has helped me to move on. HIS presence in my life has lifted the burden and pain of my life.

I thank my mother, Urmil Satya Bhushan, a well-known poetess, writer, organizer, social worker, and above all, a great humanitarian for being a constant support in my life and giving me the genes to be able to create.

I thank the two angels of my life, Ojaswini Gul and Guncha, who had come in my life so that we three can flock and fly together on this spiritual journey. Together we are

Acknowledgements

creating the new World promised by the Almighty. Thanks darlings!!!!!

At this juncture I would like to thank Aushim's mother Mrs. Asha Khetarpal whose grace and love has enveloped not only Aushim's life but many of his associates as well. She had seen the traumatic journey of his son's life without complaints and regrets. Bestowed with a small physical stature, she stands tall beside her son in his voyage of divine course. I thank her for opening her heart to me and keeping her faith in me.

I thank all the associates of Aushim, friends or foes, for opening up to me and giving me an honest opinion about him.

I thank the Sai Bhakt Parivaar of Shirdi Sai Baba Foundation for accepting me as part of this family and helping me with their uninhibited opinions.

Of course, I thank Sterling Publishers, Mr. S. K. Ghai and my editor who had the patience to go through the manuscript and suggesting necessary changes.

Last but not the least, I thank Aushim for being what he is, to remain sane even after going through what he went through, his immense energy and for allowing me to pry in his personal pains and troubles, for accepting my analysis of his life's incidences and of course having faith in me.

Thank you all.

Love and light.

Kanu Priya
March 30, 2013

Contents

	Preface	v
	Acknowledgements	viii
1.	He was different	1
2.	Guruji's endorsement	8
3.	A new life	12
4.	Happiness was short lived	16
5.	It happened again	20
6.	He had to be famous	26
7.	Aushim and sports	31
8.	Something was going to change now	40
9.	Controversy	47
10.	Another chapter	63
11.	The final blow	67
12.	The Divine and the bhakt	71

1

He was different

The fan was moving very fast. He tried to count the blades, though he knew it was not possible. He knew he can ask it to stop but he wanted it to move at the speed wished by him. Lying on the bed he could see the fast moving grey blades and deadly white ceiling. It was as if nothing else existed. He now wanted the fan to slow down. He instructed the blades to slow down. His thoughts were very powerful, concentrated; and inside his heart he knew that the fan will have to listen to him.

He told the fan, '.......... slow down – slow down – slow down' – it was a call from within. He realized that the fan's blades were now visible. It was slowing down, it was no more a continuous whirl but the three sharp grey blades were clearly visible.

He knew it – it will slow down and gradually will stop. But before it could completely stop he wanted it to start moving again. He instructed the fan not to stop but start moving – 'move – move faster....' and it obeyed him diligently. The blades started moving at a higher speed and once again the blades were not distinguishable. It was a grey whirl.

He knew it was his doing.

But no one would believe it.

To reassure himself, he instructed the fan to slow down again, 'slow-slow............slow down'.

And it once again slowed down.

He knew it will slow down.

He had done it.

He didn't have an iota of doubt that it will not obey his wish.

And then he heard his mom in the other room saying, 'what's wrong with your fan Aushim? Why is it playing such games?'

'Nothing mom', he smiled at himself. They'll never believe it, but then He knew it. He told the fan to move once again.

He had proved it to himself that it was working.

The non-living and living things had been listening to him and obeying him for a long time.

It was the human beings he had a problem with.

He had tried telling his parents and brother about what has been happening. They looked at him with such weird expression that gradually He had stopped sharing anything with them. Usually people, his friends, relatives, or teachers took him to be arrogant and conceited; though he wasn't.

It was just that he had these unusual feeling.

He could feel it but was not able to express and people around him felt he was rude.

It was difficult for him to explain because so much was going inside his head. He was never sure whether it is the truth or his imagination; also his sensitivity to criticism had made him an introvert.

Today the school results had come. Once again he felt let down by everyone and, most importantly, by his own self. He was in class X but could secure only 62% while on the other hand his brother, who was in class IX, has once again secured 90%. His father was frustrated, angry, and irritated and his mom was heartbroken.

They expect their elder son to excel in studies and in everything but he was not able to achieve what they wanted. They never compared him with his younger brother deliberately. He knew that his parents loved him immensely, but he felt helpless.

Aushim was fifteen, elder son of Mr. Purushotam Swaroop Khetarpal, the star pilot of Air India. His parents and relatives loved him a lot, as he was the first grandchild of the family. But his brother came soon. Sometimes he felt, too soon, just after a year. Aushim was a shy, introvert but very sharp child. On the other hand, his brother, Umang, was vocal, cute, charming, intelligent and a brilliant child. Everyone felt that Aushim was a quiet child. His mother worried about him, but from within Aushim knew he was DIFFERENT. He knew he has come to this world for something else and not for the mundane life his parents, relatives or other people lived. He always felt that there is some force, which compels him towards unusual things. He could talk to birds, dogs, animals, plants, trees, walls, doors and sometimes even to his books. Every time he talked through his thoughts he felt they understood and reciprocated. He would instruct them through his mind and they would follow his instructions, almost always. It was only when the doubt came, they didn't follow him. Otherwise, when he was completely sure, they always followed his instructions.

It was humans whom he couldn't understand.

They wouldn't follow him. They won't listen to him the way other objects or animals would do.

Even if Aushim didn't live in a joint family, there house was always full of people. His mother, the only sister of five very loving and caring brothers, loved family gatherings and was the most loved *bua* and *mami* to both the sides. They always had cousins staying over in their house. For Aushim, it wasn't that he had to compete only with his siblings but with all other bold and talented cousins. The whole family of Khetarpals and Butalias (his mother's side) were very close to Aushim's parents and his siblings, but he wasn't close to anyone except his younger brother, Umang, and sister, Cherié.

However, he always felt competitive towards them. Whenever they'll be sitting in the family get-togethers and there'll be talk about the future of the children, most of the children would be ready with their answers to what they want. The only answer from Aushim would be, 'I want to be big, famous and rich'. When asked about the means and the ways, usually there'll be a shrug and an answer, 'you will just see'.

Asha Khetarpal, Aushim's mother, tells us: 'Aushim was a very ambitious child. Me and my husband wanted to give our children complete freedom to take decision in their life, but at the same time, wanted them to have right values and commitments towards relationships and society. Both my younger son and daughter were very friendly with all the cousins and relatives, but Aushim was fiercely competitive and would get hurt easily on small comments. My husband at times used to worry about him; but I knew someday this child of mine would make a mark.'

Usually Aushim would know what's going to happen to people's life but he was too detached and uncomfortable with them and therefore decided not to tell anyone about these. In the beginning, he had tried to tell them but either they ridiculed him or took it as coincidence; so gradually he stopped discussing these things with others.

Today he was depressed and sad because as usual his mom was worried and his father angry. His father didn't know what to do with him. Aushim knew, very soon he will be summoned and delivered a big lecture on the importance of doing well in studies, and how important it was to do well in the Xth standard exam. That will be followed by the talk on how his father had excelled in flying and was a self-made man. No one in his father's family had achieved what his father had achieved because of his will power. Aushim had heard these stories many times.

He could never understand elders; they would either be telling stories about their past or the glories of their struggle. He was bored. He didn't want to listen to them.

He sneaked out of his house and went to the most comfortable place in this world, the pool in the club--one place where he felt he belonged. It was not that he didn't like people; more was that they didn't like him. Lying on the pool side, he dipped his hand in the cool water and suddenly memory of another day flashed through his mind.

Last year his father had taken him to Haridwar where his Guruji lived. Haridwar, one of the most holy places in India had a strange effect on him. He felt as if he has come home. The vibrations of the place, the bhaguva, bright orange dresses of the sadhus were welcoming; it was as if some past reminiscences were calling him. Meeting Guruji, Aushim had a strange effect-- as if he knew Guruji. Sitting amongst his disciples, Guruji welcomed Aushim with open arms and said, 'so finally you have come'.

There was so much love and warmth emanating from Guruji that Aushim felt drawn towards him.

His father introduced Aushim to Guruji and once again complained, 'Guruji, please give him your blessings. I am worried about him. He never studies and is always day dreaming. Please make him understand there is no life without studying.'

Aushim was embarrassed. He has not been able to make his father proud. Father was always worried about him. He didn't want that Guruji should feel bad about him, because for the first time, there was someone who could sense something special about Aushim and Aushim knew it.

Guruji asked him very lovingly, 'do you want to win the world, my son?'

He was taken aback.

These were the words he had been hearing in his mind for a long time. Guruji looked at him and smiled.

Aushim just bowed his head.

Something strange was happening inside him.

'You will, my son, someday – but not soon, late and after losing everything'. Then Guruji told him to go out and take a dip in the Holy Ganges.

Aushim was shattered, crest fallen and heartbroken.

Guruji's words had made him feel like a loser. Did Guruji also think that Aushim was no good and took him to be arrogant? He reached the ghat. It was the month of January, and the water was freezing. He wanted to do something to feel better. He dipped his hand in the water; it was cold, ice cold. He dipped it again and then told himself to see how long he can withstand it. He let the hand remain in water, he could feel the coldness… it was numbing but he was testing his will power. The coldness started reaching out to his shoulder but, again and again, Guruji's words kept coming back to him: 'You will win but not now. It will take time, a long time, and after you have lost everything'. But Aushim wanted to win now. This ice-cold water was his test. He was testing his endurance. It was becoming increasingly difficult to keep his hand in the water. He had started shivering. Cold wind was chilling him from all the sides. No one was around him in that cold evening. He could not feel the existence of his hands anymore. It was almost an hour before his father called out for him. By that time he was reaching the stage of losing his senses, but on his call he took out his hand, which had become blue. He didn't want his father to see it. He put it in his jacket's pocket. They started walking back. His father was silent and so was Aushim; both were lost in their own world.

2
Guruji's endorsement

Coming back from Haridwar, his life changed and so was his father's. He became quiet; no more would he get angry with Aushim. In fact, he became caring towards him. Many times Aushim felt his father was secretly observing him. Sometimes he felt little tender, loving gestures coming from his father.

Even in family gatherings he would notice his father defending him rather than condemning him.

Aushim never liked to eat green vegetables, especially capsicum, and invariably would push capsicum away from his plate. Usually this would cause a major scuffle between him and mom, and his father would interfere. And result would be some scolding for him. But now Aushim observed during the usual tussle between mom and him that his father just told mom, 'if he doesn't like it why do you cook it?' Mom felt hurt but Aushim was taken aback.

Guruji's endorsement

This was a major shift. Gradually there was a comfortable silence between him and his father.

But today, the result has once again brought back the rejection in him. For a long time now there were no more self doubt about himself, but he needed to know what is it that he must do with his life so that he can do what he has to do. Suddenly he felt his father's presence around, very quietly sitting beside him and looking at the pool.

He said, 'So Shimee, what do you plan to do with your life?'

Impromptu came the answer, 'make it successful.'

'But how would you do that? His father sounded worried.

'By becoming famous', answered Aushim.

'And how will you become famous?' quizzed his father.

'I don't know yet but, I am sure about that,' answered the son.

Father advised, 'fame comes with hard work, intellect and continuity of the work you are doing.'

'But I feel everything comes with will power, Papa; and I have the will, I have the intention of becoming famous and I will', argued the confident son. Father smirked, 'don't make castles in air, my son; you are day dreaming. If you really want to be famous, you must concentrate on a particular line and work hard.'

And then he went away.

Once again Aushim felt rejected and condemned. He needed something to prove that he is capable of doing something worth. He went out into the street and entered the roadside park. Sitting on the bench he saw a street dog, a new dog, because he knew all the other dogs of the locality. They were his humble, obedient servants. The dog started barking at him. Aushim looked into his eyes. He felt that the dog was listening to his thoughts. Without speaking, through his mind Aushim told him to stop - stop – stop and he stopped barking. He again told him through his thoughts – sit, sit and sit – and he sat. Then he told him again without speaking to come and sit beside him on the bench and the dog did it. Aushim felt happy and patted its back, and the dog started licking his hand. The moment Aushim conveyed anything to the dog through his thoughts, he would look into his eyes for few seconds and then do it. Finally, Aushim told him to go. The dog looked at him with lot of hurt, but eventually went away.

Aushim felt good.

It works with everyone and everything except humans.

But one day it'll work with them as well. 'I know, Papa, I know it, it'll work'.

He was happy and came back home smiling. He felt like a winner.

Entering the drawing room he heard his mom speaking in a concerned voice to his father: 'But what exactly Guruji had said about Shimmy, please tell me clearly.'

Aushim knew it was wrong to overhear, but, it was too important. He had to know; so he hid behind the curtain.

'What's it you want to know?' Father sounded little agitated.

'Everything. I'm his mom. I have the right to know everything. I have noticed some changes in you. Since the time you have come back from Haridwar you are very quiet and at times concerned. Please tell me what is the matter?'

Father said lovingly to his mom, 'Sit Asha, don't be worried, everything will be fine'.

Guruji's endorsement

He held her hand and made her sit beside him. These tender and loving moments were very few in his parents' life. Witnessing one made him feel very good. He felt like an intruder but wanted to know what they were talking as it was about him. His father was speaking now.

'Listen Asha, Guruji said that we are very lucky. Shimmi is a very special soul. He'll will be very famous one day and make us proud, but...'

'But what...?' Asked his mom.

'Only if he survives his 42nd birthday, till 42 his life will be marred by great difficulties and tragedies. It's going to be a turbulent journey because of his own stubbornness, but if he survives his 42nd birthday, he'll find a path – and then there'll be no looking back. By 49 he'll gain lot of power and energies and would have finished off all his Karmas. At 54 it'll be a different life and different world for him.'

Aushim was awe struck, but instantly knew it to be true. He knew he was going to be famous.

His mom had started crying, 'but what tragedies and difficulties Guruji was talking about!' Father said, 'he never explained! He only said nobody can help him, it is his due and also it is his test; but don't worry. Guruji said, he'll endure it and will win all the battles'.

Mom wailed, 'but why the battles? Is there a solution? Can something be done, some puja, yagya, anushthan, or any 'mantra jaap?' Father said, 'Guruji says, nothing will work, but your prayers will. Also, try to contain him because he'll be very head strong.'

This was more than enough for him. Aushim moved away. He knew that what he had heard was true. He was different and that's it.

3
A new life

His life changed. He became more confident and vocal. He started answering in his class. The urge to prove, to move ahead remained. Although his marks didn't improve much, he always felt that he was better than others. After passing out, his brother joined the All India Institute of Medical Sciences and he joined Hindu College for his B.Com Honours.

One of the most important incidents in his life was his first love.

Although he had started noticing girls but he was too shy to interact with them. But as his confidence grew, so did his courage.

Even though he deeply respected the fairer sex, he was never able to have a relationship with them. On the other hand, his brother, Umang, was very popular amongst girls and had many casual relationships. However, Aushim was

A new life

looking for someone he could dependent on, could trust and could truly love.

The first person he met in the college was a warm and friendly English girl named Christine. She came from a traditional family in Nottingham. She had come here to pursue her study in literature and was deeply inclined towards the Indian cultures and traditions. They became friends instantly. Christine loved his soft and gentle nature, whereas Aushim was attracted to her simplicity and grace.

They started going out. On several of their dates, they had deep conversations about religion, mythology and culture of India.

Christine was fascinated by the Indian gods, especially Lord Krishna.

Then an incident happened, which made Aushim realize that he knew almost nothing about his own culture. Usually Christine wore western clothes but that day she came to college in traditional Indian attire -- bright yellow kurta, orange salwaar and bandhini duppatta with lot of colorful bangles. She had mehndi on her hands and wore a small red *bindi* on her forehead. Aushim was unable to take his eyes off her. That day she looked divine and pure, especially when she started talking about Krishna and Radha's love. Watching her talk about Krishna and his philosophy in itself was a delight for him.

'Krishna was not just a king or a God, but he was the perfect being. One can adore him in all his forms: enjoy his pranks and adorable games as a child; express awe over his heroic deeds as a youngster and listen in rapt attention to his courses about dharma as an adult."

'Undoubtedly, he is the perfect man. The most romantic lover, savior of the masses, best strategist for warfare; but not for the war outside, instead, the war within. And above all, he is the biggest friend of every living being on this earth" she exclaimed.

"You seem to know a lot about Krishna. How did it happen?" Asked Aushim mischievously. "Actually, this is the real reason why I came to India. I'd read an article on him, which I couldn't forget. So, I researched a lot on Krishna and finally decided to know more about him from his own people."

He was stunned; how could a girl from a foreign land know more than him about his favorite god?

"Oh god, enough! I am not an encyclopedia on Lord Krishna, Aushim! And what is this craze? Why you are suddenly so obsessed with him?" questioned Aushim's mother in frustration. Since the past three hours, Aushim had been grilling his mother about Lord Krishna. Questions were like "what time was he born?" "Was his favorite food only butter or he liked something else also?" And they were endless. This truly haunted Aushim's mother now. "How come you want to know about Gods and our culture? Trying to impress someone, bhaiya?' teased his sister playfully.

'Of course. Aushim never does anything without a purpose, right Aushim? This time it is to impress his *firangi* girlfriend," remarked Umang who had just returned from his cricket practice.

'Which firang? Whose girlfriend? Can someone please tell me what is going on?" Shouted Cherié. Aushim's mother, who till now was resting on the sofa, exhausted from Aushim's cruel questioning, suddenly got up. The scenario in the living room for her was something like this: Cherié was teasing

A new life

Aushim with raised eyebrows; Aushim was red enough to look like an expensive tomato while Umang was staring at Aushim with a horror-stricken face. Then she heard Umang say something which truly traumatized her, "don't tell me that you plan to marry a firang, Aushim!"

"Oh My God! First he drills me about Krishna's life, then he plans on marrying a firang! What are you trying to do? Slowly torture me to death?" Aushim made his mom sit on a chair, gave her some water and after letting her fume about how she would have the worst *bahu* possible, he calmly explained, "listen mom, these two have gone mad. No one is getting married. No bahu is coming. Remember, I'd told you about Christine, my college friend. Well, she wanted to know something about Krishna, and I opted to help her. That's all". Finally some peace settled in the house.

He finally got some good advice from his mother. She told him that the ISKCON temple's bookshop had the best books on Lord Krishna. Following his mother's advice, Aushim took Christine to ISKCON. After buying the books, Aushim and Christine sat near the fountains and continued talking about Lord Krishna. The beautiful temple and the peaceful atmosphere made their discussion an even deeper one. Aushim realized that unlike Christine, who was enchanted by the love of Radha and Krishna, he was more attracted by Krishna's philosophy.

Slowly but steadily, Aushim opened up to Christine. She was the sunshine of his life. He was completely in love with her. Her beauty, her smile, her innocence and her complete faith in him made him feel complete for the first time in his life. He finally felt at peace with himself and with his life. He forgot all the rejections and condemnation of the past. Her care and love was all he needed. At last, he had found happiness.

4

Happiness was short lived

Suddenly, Aushim's life took a dramatic turn.

Christine was detected with Blood Cancer.

The eighteen year old who had once dreamt to spend her entire life as a true Krishna bhakt, now had only four months to live. Her rapidly deteriorating condition made Aushim desperately pray for a miracle.

He went to ISKCON to sit in silence and ponder over the turn of events. As Christine's family wanted her to spend her last days with them, she packed her bags to go back. Within a few days, Christine left. By this time, Aushim had become completely numb and had stopped reacting. After her departure, Aushim was silent for a month. As he had always been a quiet and introvert child, no one in his family noticed his silence. On the other hand, his father's life had changed radically within this few months.

Out of the blue, his father was detected with a severe problem in his ears that affected his work as a pilot. Being a pilot in Air India, for him, life held no meaning without flying. However, the problem in his ears was worsening, and one day, his father was asked to move over to ground duty. His father was shaken but he refused to give up. In spite of all his efforts, he couldn't revive his flying duties.

Disheartened, his father opted for voluntary retirement. However, this decision turned out to be extremely tough for the whole family, especially for Aushim. His father, a self-made man, was never an easy person to handle. If 'not flying' was difficult for him to accept, sitting at home was even harder. More than the financial insecurity, it was the feeling of being useless that made his and his family's' life miserable at home. By this time Umang had shifted to the hostel. Thus, it was Aushim, his mother and his younger sister Cherié who had to take the brunt. Aushim, who was already going through the loss of his first love, was not ready to take the constant bickering of his father. His mother, who was Aushim's biggest support, seeing her husband's condition, was more sympathetic and caring towards the husband. Cherié, a beautiful, vivacious young girl, at the moment was also trying to charter her life in the field of modeling.

One thing about his parents was they had given all the three children complete confidence and independence to plan their careers. But as a normal Indian middle-class parents they had their apprehensions about the choices. In fact, when he looked back he realized that they were very supportive of both Umang and Cherié, because, both of them were very clear, open, focused and hard working towards their plans. He was the only one different as they didn't have any clear idea about his ambitions. He himself was sure that he would do business, but was not sure on the type of the business. As he was always a quiet person, his father thought Aushim was not smart enough. Coming from a humble, middle-class background, thought process and surroundings, his father was wary of people involved in business. He had always thought that a businessman has to be a sharp shooter and a smart talker. Now, with his own frustrations and insecurities the senior Khetarpal made Aushim's life hell.

Aushim's mom says: 'That was the worst period of my life! Though Aushim had not talked much about his girlfriend, I knew he was depressed and very sad. Aushim had never learned how to express love; he only knew how to accept it. Seeing him sharing love with the girl had made me comfortable. But now I could feel his pain. On one side there was my husband who was going through turmoil. He was not a man who suffered in silence; when he suffered, the whole house suffered. Umang was in hostel and Cherié was not a person who would be daunted by anything; instead, her pleasant presence was like a balm to me and my husband. But during his illness the differences between my husband and Aushim got worsened. There was no one to be blamed, both had the similar personalities and could never handle losses. I had expected Aushim to be more restrained as he was the elder son. But I realized he was a complex and different person. His arrogant and rude behavior at times not only hurt my husband but me as well. As a mother I could never realize how siblings, children of the same parents, brought up in the same environment can be so different in their response to similar situations.'

Losing Christine had awakened the rebel in Aushim. He was rebelling against everything; against friends, against his parents, against his siblings and also against God. He hated everyone; he was thrashing and looking out for love and comfort. But there was no one to turn to; his brother and sister were busy in taking care of their parents and also making their own careers, no cousin with whom he could confide in and no friend he could gel with.

5
It happened again

Going through these traumatic times he fell in love again. She was his neighbor and was also going through her heartbreak. They bonded well.

He was shocked at himself. When he had lost Christine, he thought he will never be able to love anyone, but he was in love again! He understood the human mind for the first time. It goes where it finds happiness. Whichever experience has given the mind peace, love, and happiness, it'll seek for that experience. But this relationship was different; his relationship with Alpna was developed based on pain. Both of them had experienced the pain of loss and were looking for comfort and healing. Initially the experience was profound and comforting, but gradually comparisons started developing. He couldn't find the same completeness which he had felt in his past experience. Alpna started having complaints about his personality. They started having verbal arguments more frequently. On the other hand, breaking down of his father at home was driving him crazy.

Aushim was shocked to realize how a man without work or position loses his self confidence and self worth.

His father, the handsome, jolly, confident and proud man was becoming a slave of his own insecurities and miseries. He realized that a man should never retire without planning something for himself. It was not lack of money as he had planned his financial future very well but it was his lack of position and power that made him so miserable. In three years he became just a shadow of what he was. He was becoming cynical, critical, angry and very difficult to handle. His fights with his father were becoming a regular feature at home.

His mom, with lot of patience and self control was trying very hard to bring more color and involvement in her husband's life. She requested him to start some business to remain occupied. But his father's stubbornness and misplaced pride didn't let him do that.

On the other hand, Aushim was raring to go. Anyone who's reading this book might feel it is going so fast -- situations are moving at a very fast pace but that's the way he was. He was a man in a hurry, he wanted to do things fast. He was racing against time. He wanted to achieve everything fast. Constant fights with Alpna and bickering at home were making him mad. Still, being with Alpna gave him an anchor. He always felt he can come back to her for the reassurance and they would always make-up. He came from a background where the value system teaches you that relationships are forever. At the age of 21, he was already thinking of being with her for ever but another shock was round the corner.

Once watching TV together, Umang, who was more of a friend than a brother, casually asked, 'are you serious about Alpna?'

Umang being a light hearted and focused person was cool and casual about his relationships. But he also knew Aushim's intensity about relationship. They shared a silent, acceptable relationship and had mutual respect for each other. A question like this coming from Umang made him take a pause.

'Why? What's wrong in being serious?' asked Aushim defensively.

Umang causally said, 'because, I think she is not. So, you better check it out with her, otherwise there'll again be a heartbreak.'

'How would you know? You don't even talk to her. Or, is it that secretly you might be fancying her?' He asked the tongue-in-cheek question to Umang.

'Forget about it. You are insane! I don't need my brother's handouts as girlfriends! It's just that she was at our fest with my senior, Abhishek; and ever since I have seen them together in the hostel and in the campus as well. Why don't you confront her and ask straight away?' Suggested Umang.

Aushim couldn't believe it.

But nevertheless, he straight away asked Alpna about it.

She openly confessed to her new relationship with Abhishek, whom she had met in the college fest and he had fallen in love with her instantly.

Confronting Alpna was an earth-shaking experience. He was aghast at her casual acceptance. 'Alpna, he fell in love, not you. You were already in a relationship, with me, if you remember.' Aushim accused.

'Let's face it Aushim. You call it a relationship? I already feel so old and tired with you. Every time we meet, we either fight, sulk or talk about your ambitions. I'm tired and sick of being with you'.

He was angry now, 'you mean to say you are in relationship with both of us? Whatever might be happening between us, Alpna, still we have been together'.

Alpna was really angry now. 'We are not married, Aushim, that we have to be together even if we can't stand each other. No, I'm through with you, good you talked, because I was going to talk about it.'

He felt something breaking inside; it could not be happening, "don't say this Alpna, I love you and we do understand each other. We have our differences but we can always sort them out. I care a lot for you. Believe me, we can handle this.'

These tender words made her quiet but then holding his hand she said, 'You are one of the best guys I've met, Aushim. You are a thorough gentleman; but you are too focused on your needs, and your needs and ambitions are different in life. I want stability. You don't have a future. Abhishek's career is set. He'll be a doctor in a year or so. His parents are NRIs. He is the only son. I have a future there. Neither your career nor your family's status suit my parents aspirations for me, and I realize if I've a right to choose my partner, I should choose the best of the two. Sorry for all this but forget about me and all the best. And she just walked off.

He couldn't believe it. This was not happening to him! He felt too tired to react. He just sat in a DTC Mudrika Bus that goes on a roundtrip around Delhi and didn't even realize that he was in it. His whole life came back to him as a flash back. In that one-hour ride he saw himself as a loser at every step of his life. The special powers he had experienced were of no use as they didn't bring prosperity, love or acceptance of people.

There was something rebelling in him.

He wanted to completely lash out but this time his anger was not directed to anyone.

Suddenly he was not angry with people around him.

It was as if they didn't exist.

He was like a slow burning agarbatti, without any light or fragrance.

He was calm and quiet from outside but inside something just cracked.

He came back home.

Umang was still at home, maybe waiting for Aushim as he knew Aushim will be hurt.

Their eyes met and Umang could make out what would have transpired between them. Aushim just slumped on the sofa. Umang got orange juice and putting the glass in his hands, said, 'listen Aushim, how long will you live in this fool's paradise? Why are you chasing these girls? They are nothing. See, you wanted to be famous, then work on that, believe me one day you'll be famous, all the money and girls will follow you.'

'Let's go and watch a movie.'

After coming back from the movie, Umang went back to his hostel but something clicked inside Aushim. Umang's words kept coming back to him.

He closed his door and started watching movies.

He didn't want to think.

He had a whole library of Amitabh Bachchan's films in which the hero is at loggerhead with the society. Every film was like his own story but he watched them as a rational viewer. He saw the arrogance of Vijay, the character portrayed by the actor coming out from every rejection. For three days he confined himself in that room and watched those films round-the-clock; these films were like catharsis.

He could see his life clearly now. He realized he will not be daunted anymore by rejections; in fact, he will not look for any acceptance anymore. He understood the need to be focused and working to win. He wanted to work, stay focused, earn lots of money and become famous.

6
He had to be famous

THIS WAS DECIDED.

HE HAD TO BE FAMOUS!!!

After three days of being on the constant diet of Hindi movies and also the videos of Mohamed Ali, which had inspired him a lot about the strategies that are needed to win, he had learned the art of being persuasive, confident and manipulative. So, when he came out to the world again he was a different man.

A man out to win!

He wasn't afraid of losing any more as he didn't have anything to lose. He had learnt the art to win. He learnt how to project confidence.

He took up a job in marketing. He had realized that the first thing he needed was a breakthrough to create his network and that is why he took up a regular job. In Aushim's entire life these six months were the only time he had taken up a job, and within the first month, he became the best salesperson of the company. Suddenly, he was an outspoken, smart person who created magic with his plans. His clients were happy as he could convince them not only about the products he was selling—there was something more than that. He became the blue-eyed sales person for most of his clients.

More than his products, he could sell them ideas about their products.

Aushim had an ability to see beyond, the clairvoyance, which he couldn't understand at that point but his clients were impressed by him because he would create visions they could not even comprehend. They became his friends. By the end of six months he was in partnership with his company. He was earning a lot of money now. He was moving above the social ladder. Suddenly his life was brighter from every side. Umang was planning to move over to America for further studies, Cherié's career as a model was growing and she was also working in a traveling agency.

Only sad part was that their father was detected with cancer, and their mother was doing everything to make him feel better.

Another turning point in his life was round the corner. The company he was partner with had to be shut down as promoters had a fight and they split; it didn't come as a shock to him as he was ready to move on his own.

By this time, he had enough confidence and cartel of clients in his kitty.

He had money in his bank.

He had courage in his heart.

He had dreams in his eyes.

He had plans in his mind.

He had trust in his powers.

From his childhood Aushim had been interested in sports and had played tennis at National level. During his schooldays he had traveled all over India for the tournaments. He always felt bad at the condition of sportspersons in India. He always felt that the field of sports has been ignored badly in the country. He was passionate about creating awareness on the importance of sports in people's life.

By this time he wanted to nurture young talents in sports and with this vision soon opened his own sports academy.

Radiant Tennis Academy opened in October 1987 and within one month, in November, his father died.

This has happened with Aushim again and again in his life.

With his every achievement or personal glory came the moments of great personal loss. He couldn't comprehend the loss of his father. He felt cheated. Now when the moment had come for his father to be proud of him, he was not there; as if he had turned his face completely from Aushim's success.

He gave himself completely to the academy. This brought in another aspect of his personality.

He had a profound effect of his mother's rearing which became visible during the academy days. Children of bureaucrats, stars, models, and TV personalities were attending his academy. The way he nurtured and groomed them was surprising to him as well.

Deep inside he was a very caring and loving person. Bureaucrats, professionals and advertisers were enamored and enchanted by this young, dynamic, soft spoken but intense young man.

The academy produced many champions in the field of tennis for the country.

Aushim always felt that India should work in different sports rather than just cricket, and he became instrumental in promoting not only tennis but billiards and snooker as well.

Many young champs were being trained at the academy.

Aushim roped in Balram Singh, one of the selectors of present Indian team and also one of India's top tennis players in the 1960s as the coach of his academy. He also coached the Indian team from 1989 to 1992. To him goes the credit of producing many top international level players such as Rohit Rajpal and Mark Ferreira.

Balram Singh, a soft spoken, dedicated coach looks back at those times with lot of fondness but regret as well, according to him,

'Aushim had his calling in sports; he was not just a very good national level tennis player but was a great organizer. He had spark and vision; he was instrumental in bringing Indian tennis to international foray. Radiant was the best as it was the first of its kind, fresh and full of passion just because of Aushim. He would create so much more into the sports than just the sport itself. We were a great team and produced many champions who are still leading sports in the country. But Aushim just got involved in too many things, I feel sad not for Aushim but for the field of sports because if he would have continued, Indian sports scenario would have been completely different. He had it in him to make it big for sports and sportspersons in India'.

For Aushim, who was rearing to go and wanted more for these sports champs in terms of national and international recognition, the field created many opportunities.

As his social circle now included many sportspersons, socialites, models, designers and elites of the society, he decided to venture into an arena which was completely unexplored in India till then. As he had trust in his intuition, he knew he will be good in this venture and this will work out.

7
Aushim and sports

This was the time when he met Michael Ferreira, the famous Billiards player, who won the World Billiards Championship four times.

A true champion, Michael had created history by becoming the first amateur to make a 1000 point break in billiards In December 1978.

Apart from being a great player, Michael has been well known for a true rebellion who has always pleaded equal facilities and encouragement to other sports and games apart from cricket.

In Michael, Aushim found a true partner.

For this veteran billiards player he was a man who had the burning desire and also the all consuming passion to take other sports like billiards and snooker to a different dimension.

Together they were a deadly combination.

Aushim ventured into the world of sports promotion.

It was an unexplored, unheard field.

People were not aware that the popularity of the sportsperson can be utilized in the big promotional events. Also, placing and promotion of these national players for the endorsements was never thought of at that time. Aushim became instrumental in bringing in all the international sporting events to India.

He worked hard to open his own company in sports promotion. Radiant Sports Management started its operation in

Aushim was happy. He was passionate about promotion of sports in the country.

Everyone could feel the vibrations and energies in his presence. He worked round the clock. He loved working. Sporting events other than cricket were becoming a reality in India.

After the death of his father, his mother had stood by him. Now she came in open for his support. He was the youngest achiever of that year. This was also becoming the best period of his life. Umang was in U.S. and Cherié was travelling a lot because of her various modeling assignments.

With the complete attention and support of his mother, he started moving ahead in his various venture.

He was surprised and also enchanted by his mother's acumen for businesses' nitty-gritty. When he was busy outside handling the events, press conferences, parties for the promoters and other public functions, she, with great efficiency handled the backend. They were a great team. At night, after coming back home, she would listen to him for hours about his plans, his apprehension, and his anxieties with patience and then softly advise him about the things he could do. She was the best sounding board he could have as she understood all his hidden desires to win and succeed.

He was instrumental in changing the face of sports promotion and sporting events and in popularizing them in the country; he was doing very well for his company.

When contacted, Michael Ferreira was nostalgic about the times spent with Aushim. He sounded little wary about how the relationship had diverted but when digged deeper he had fond memories of their partnership of those seven eight years.

He said, 'Aushim was an enigma, full of innovative ideas, had extra ordinary ability to convince people and generate sponsorships. He changed the profile of the game. He had a certain knack for predictions and invariably they would come true. Once we were in London and were in a shabby hotel. Looking into the mirror in the hotel room, he promised me that next time we'll be the state guests and would stay in a palatial hotel, and true to his words, that's exactly what happened. He made tennis, billiards and snooker the most happening and in thing. He gets credit to bring in money and glamour to sports but somewhere he went overboard, got lost in this unending quest; sometimes the financial deals became difficult. I feel- he ate more than he could chew, and that's sad for not only him but for the sports as well.'

Finally he felt he had found his calling. He was climbing the social ladder very fast. He was the youngest sports promoter in the country.

Media was becoming his biggest support.

He was young, rich and available. Suddenly all the celebrities were his friends. As he was instrumental in bringing sportsperson and film stars together his home had become a hub for all of them. They used to stay with him. His mom was the most beautiful, graceful and caring host. Be it the young upcoming sports newcomers from his academy, established sports stars of international fame or Bollywood stars, models or singers, he knew most of them and vice-versa. To this small community of celebrities, he, a humble, soft spoken but a successful businessman, was a rarity. As his business was around these celebrities, he really cared for them and took extreme care for their comforts and promotion as their growth and popularity was beneficial to his work. It was a win-win situation for all, and he had the knack of creating the right kind of promotion for his people as he had complete faith in their talent and believed that they deserve all the popularity.

Rohit Rajpal, a national level tennis player and now a selector of Indian team is the product of Radiant sports academy. Looking back at those times, he became really nostalgic, 'that was the best time of our life, we were all from different schools, I found Aushim really passionate and dynamic as a promoter. He would be very enthusiastic and never give up. Aushim had become more of a family friend. Everyone at home was very fond of him. He was all for winning. He introduced many film stars in the promotion of the sports, and best part was that he was not just a promoter but himself was a player, hence understood the psychology of the players. I remember once for a benefit match one of the players fell sick, he was teamed up with Preity Zinta. We were all in a fix but without thinking twice, Aushim jumped in his place and won the match. I wish he had stayed with the sports, it would have been a different story."

Life was again blissful after a very long time.

He was the most available and eligible bachelor. There was a long string of social attachments and then cordial break offs. His friends and relatives were looking to get him married.

He was 29 and already a big success. He was on the front pages of all sports and film magazines. Every TV channel talked about his success. He featured in many shows as the youngest achiever.

Then Anya came in his life.

One of his friends, Amita, introduced him to Anya. She was the most graceful and well-mannered women he had met. But she had a past. She was already divorced and was trying to come out of a relationship with a very powerful industrialist.

Anya was like a 'dream come true' for Aushim --a sweet, simple, yet graceful and very sophisticated girl. She was a rare gem. He was amazed how her husband had let her go; because, she was an asset. He fell in love with her. She also loved him but was very confused with her life. The relationship with the industrialist was not completely off. He was madly in love with her but couldn't marry her as his wife had refused to give a divorce. Anya got along very well with Aushim's mom. Asha and Anya hit off instantly. She understood him completely. She was the only one who could bring down his temper. His evenings became beautiful. She planned every outing so tastefully that all the day's tension would lift off. Once again love bloomed in his life, it had a silver lining. Anya and Cherié also got along very well. Aushim and Anya would go for long drives till two in the morning. He was not a party man; neither was she, but she understood his professional and social responsibility and was a perfect companion for every occasion. Everything had become perfect.

Suddenly a series of incidences came crashing in and once again his life saw great upheavals.

This time tragedy struck him in the most cruel, gruesome and unexpected manner.

One night he was sleeping in his room and Cherié and mom in theirs. A notorious gang of robbers entered their house through the balcony, killed Cherié with a kullari and took whatever jewelry and cash they could.

Unexpectedly, there was no commotion in the house that particular night. A house, which was always full of family and friends, unfortunately had only three occupants that night.

They came to know about the robbery and killing in the morning.

His mom went into a shock. He couldn't comprehend what has happened. Suddenly police and media persons thronged their place.

This was the biggest news the next day and following week.

From top politicians and bureaucrats to celebrities attended the cremation and the proceedings.

As Cherié was a popular model, the story of her killing remained alive in the media for a long time.

But his life was shattered once again.

Umang came from U.S.

Mom went into a shell.

On top of it these there were rumors doing the round that the killing was the result of his animosity with some powerful people. Another such rumor which did the rounds was that he got her sister killed so that he can gain publicity and sympathy. He was simply appalled at the audacity of the rumors. Everyone started advising him and Anya to get married as this will bring his mom out of her reverie. Umang was also of the same opinion. But Anya was in doubts. The past was catching up with her. The industrialist who was in love with her knew about their friendship and had started threatening her that he'll get Aushim killed. Anya was afraid for him and completely confused. They had a long chat about their future. He wanted to get married but he could see she wasn't ready.

As he was the leading sports promoter in the country and the most happening man around, he sent Anya and her mom to London to take a break and think about her decision.

This was the last straw in the tensed situation.

His mother had gone to U.S.

Anya was in London and still very confused and indecisive.

Though a patient man by nature, he was becoming impatient with his life. Socially he needed a wife now as his career was growing at a fast pace, and then he met his future wife at a social function. She was from the hospitality industry. They hit off instantly. She was graceful yet simple. He liked her simplicity. She was trying to come out of a broken relationship. They met few times socially. And then he got the biggest jerk of his life when Anya called up and told him the decision that she didn't want to marry him.

By this time he was tired. This rejection was something he was not ready to take. Too much was happening too fast in his life.

He was at the top, literally. He proposed his new friend. She accepted heartily. He called mom back and as he was in a hurry, they got married within a month.

Their marriage was the most talked about marriage of the year. All the news channels and newspapers covered the marriage. It was a gala affair.

Their married life started off pretty nicely. His wife completely dedicated herself to his life. Unfortunately, his mother and she didn't hit off very well and within few years, they moved out of his mom's home. By this time he had quite a few properties in Delhi. His work was as taxing and tough but he was still successful.

He was doing very well in his business but was always worried as his mom was living alone. As he had discomfort in his mind about leaving mom, he started having differences at home. With the kind of life he had led, he became quiet arrogant and temperamental. He started leaving home every morning after a heated discussion with his wife. At the same time his business started going down, his promoters and advertisers started creating problems. To make up for the losses, he made wrong decisions and things started crumbling.

The beginning of 1995 saw another debacle of his life. The events he had planned couldn't take place on time and the advertisers started backing out. He tried to salvage the situations but everything started going wrong.

It was as if luck changed its face completely.

*There are Believers... and non believers.
...and we all become believers*

Aushim Khetarpal's

SHIRDI
SAI BABA

A Film By Deepak Balraj Vij

With Baba's Blessings

Sai Bhakta

Aushim Khetarpal

A SHIRDI SAI BABA FOUNDATION PRESENTATION

Shooting of film Shirdi Sai Baba 2001

Talking to Suresh Oberoi and Deepak Balraj

Animated film on Shirdi Sai Baba to spread love, brotherhood

The Shirdi Sai Baba Foundation is set to release an animated movie Shirdi Sai Baba, the first on his rich voyage, an official said Monday. The film aims at spreading love among viewers. "We are extremely excited about releasing the movie. Shirdi Sai Baba is the incarnation of god. He taught equality, brotherhood and love to the society. These animated stories and teachings of Sai Baba will definitely help to implant brotherhood and love among children and elders as well," said Aushim Khetrapal, chief founder of the Shirdi Sai Baba Foundation. Khetrapal, the movie's producer, has rendered his voiceover for a few sequences. The movie, which will release January 2012, revolves around key sequences, teachings and incidents written in Sai Satcharitra. It highlights Sai Baba's divine power and mystical charm, which still generates thrill among the devotees. A combination of mythology and technology, the movie promises entertainment with dollops of animation and special effects. Produced by Orient Tradelink and conceived by Shirdi Sai Baba Foundation, the film contains 17 chapters of Sai Satcharitra, written by Hemadpanth. Shirdi Sai Baba Foundation (SSBF), based in New Delhi, runs with the objective of spreading the teachings of Shirdi Sai Baba among masses, establish Sai temples and hospitals, as well as programmes for child protection. Last month, the foundation had released a comic book on the life and teachings of Sai Baba. It generated a positive response, selling over 50,000 copies within a month

Animated film made by SSBF to be released soon on Shirdi Sai Baba

In Meadow Brook School in Delhi

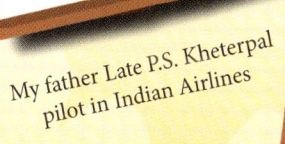
My father Late P.S. Kheterpal pilot in Indian Airlines

When he went to St. Columbas School

Om Allah shooting in Vrindavan

With Daler Mehindi, BR Shetty Chairman, UAE Exchange at Abu Dhabi Cricket concert (2006)

With Muthaiya Murlidharan & Mahela Jaiwardene (1998)

With Mahela Jaiwardene as his celebrity client (1998)

Performing live in Abu Dhabi Stadium in 2006 in front of 30000 audience (2006)

Shooting of Sai Baba at Shirdi

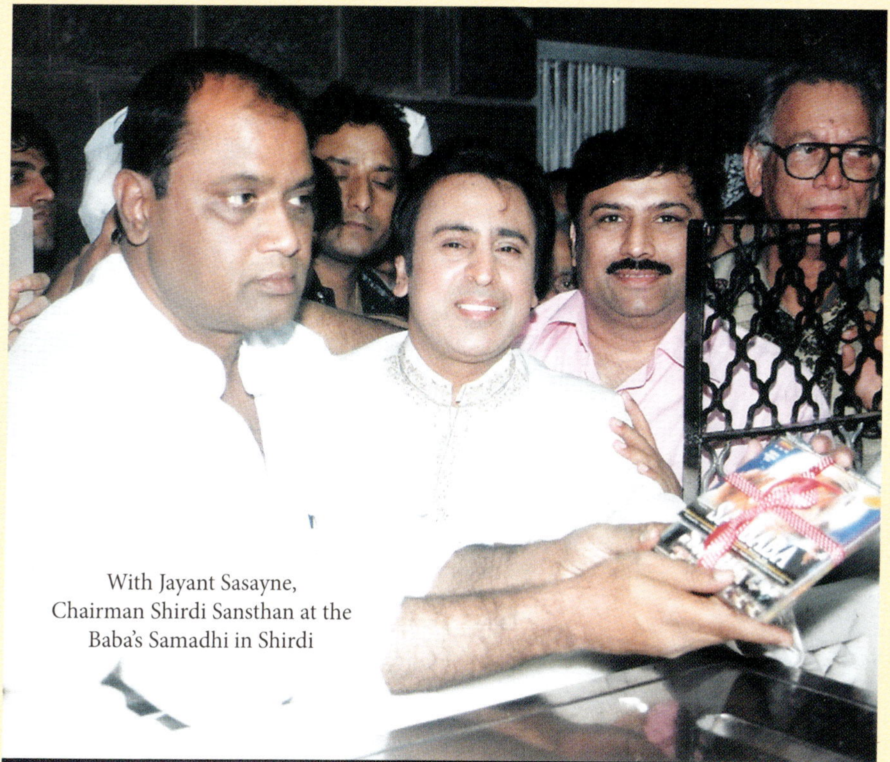

With Jayant Sasayne,
Chairman Shirdi Sansthan at the
Baba's Samadhi in Shirdi

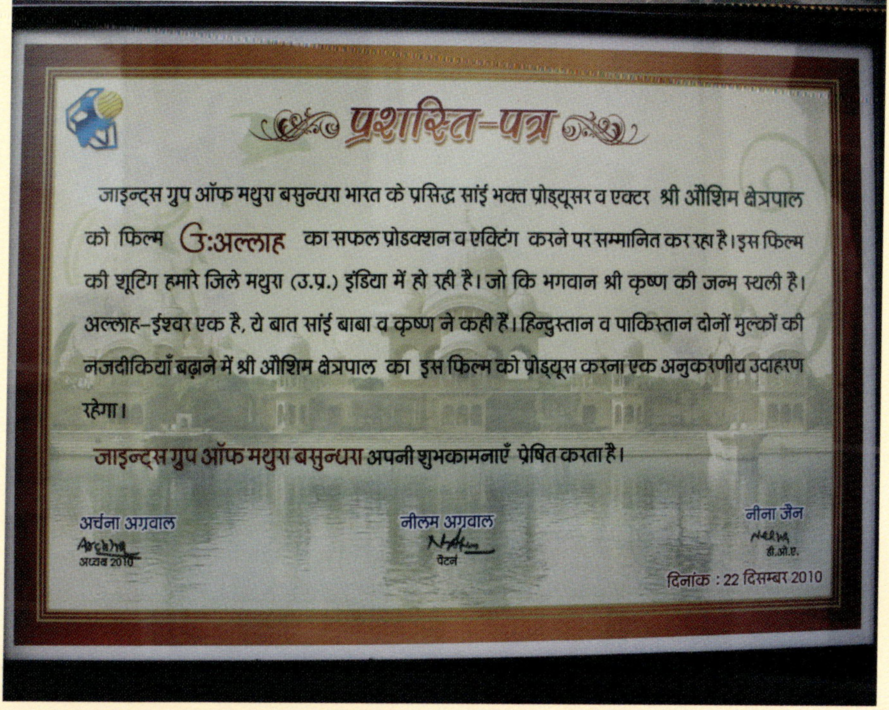

प्रशस्ति-पत्र

जाइन्ट्स ग्रुप ऑफ मथुरा बसुन्धरा भारत के प्रसिद्ध सांई भक्त प्रोड्यूसर व एक्टर श्री औशिम क्षेत्रपाल को फिल्म ॐअल्लाह का सफल प्रोडक्शन व एक्टिंग करने पर सम्मानित कर रहा है। इस फिल्म की शूटिंग हमारे जिले मथुरा (उ.प्र.) इंडिया में हो रही है। जो कि भगवान श्री कृष्ण की जन्म स्थली है। अल्लाह-ईश्वर एक है, ये बात सांई बाबा व कृष्ण ने कही हैं। हिन्दुस्तान व पाकिस्तान दोनों मुल्कों की नजदीकियाँ बढ़ाने में श्री औशिम क्षेत्रपाल का इस फिल्म को प्रोड्यूस करना एक अनुकरणीय उदाहरण रहेगा।

जाइन्ट्स ग्रुप ऑफ मथुरा बसुन्धरा अपनी शुभकामनाएँ प्रेषित करता है।

अर्चना अग्रवाल
अध्यक्ष 2010

नीलम अग्रवाल
पैटर्न

नीना जैन
डी.ओ.ए.

दिनांक : 22 दिसम्बर 2010

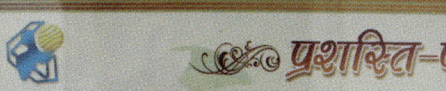

Prashasist Patra given by Mathura Authority

THE TIMES OF

Businessman leaves everything for Divine search

Faith in reality

TELEVISION Aushim Khetrapal on his new series on Sai Baba

In the season of reality television, here comes one more. Aushim Khetrapal, known for his diverse interests ranging from sports management to acting and singing, has come up with a series on Shirdi Sai Baba on a Sony channel.

Already several films and serials have been made on him, so what's different this time? "True, in fact one of my serials on Sai Baba has been on air for quite some time. The difference is, this time we have come up with a real-ity series on Sai Baba. Instances will be shown where people have recovered from difficult circumstances because of their faith in Sai Baba," says Aushim.

Dramatised version

Aushim says, "We will have dramatised versions of each in-

TELE-PATHY? Scenes from Khetrapal's serial on Sai Baba

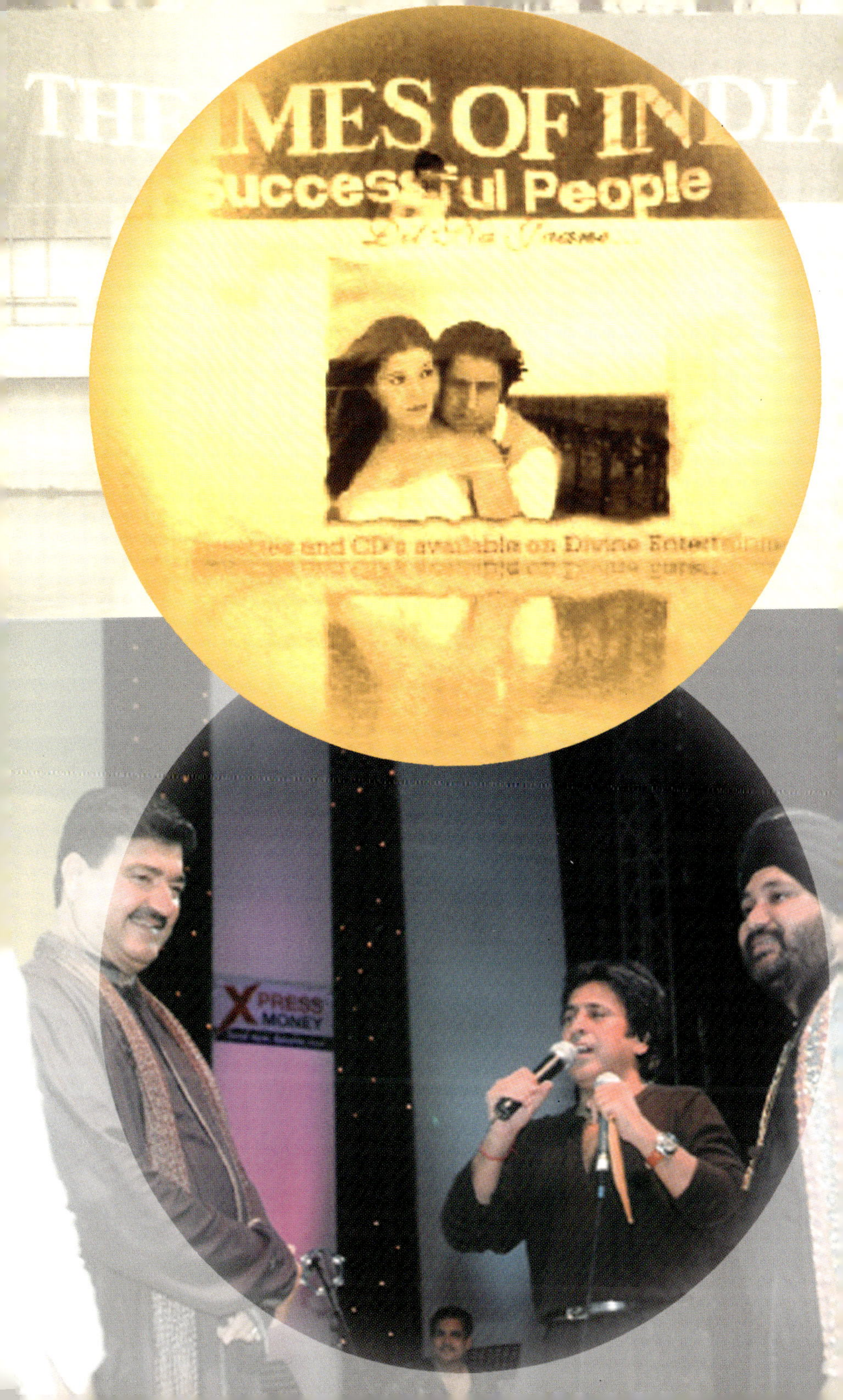
MES OF INDIA
ul People
XPRESS MONEY

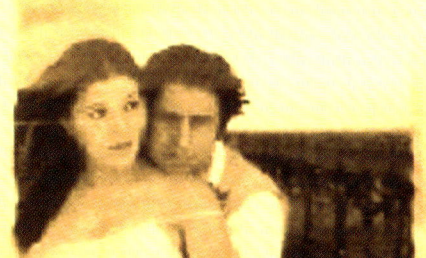

Controversy at its best

Calm and Composed delivering a discourse

Model of proposed temple at Vrindavan

Rajnath Singh, President BJP releasing a pictre book Shirdi Sai Baba

THE HINDU

Today's Paper » NATIONAL » NEW DELHI

Published: September 21, 2011 00:00 IST | Updated: September 21, 2011 04:03 IST

The truth about match fixing

Madhur Tankha
Upcoming film Om Allah brings out real life story of ex-sports promoter

Aushim Khetarpal

Former sports promoter turned film-maker Aushim Khetarpal feels that his upcoming Indo-Pakistani film Om Allahwill put to rest all speculation surrounding his involvement in the match fixing controversy during the late 1990s. The film depicts Aushim's real life story of being accused of match fixing and finally getting his name cleared. Aushim, who is also an actor, says the film also depicts the plight of three Pakistani cricket players whose names were dragged in the spot-fixing controversy last year. "My film will take viewers to the real incident that occurred in 1999-2000 during the cricket series between India and England," he says. As he was a sports promoter, he had met a former England all-rounder. But the cricketer accused him of match fixing in an interview he gave to a tabloid. Aushim says it was a concocted story but the media splashed a series of news stories consecutively on the front page for 14 days. "This badly tarnished my reputation and the case was investigated by the Scotland Yard. Eventually I was given a clean chit. From there on, I wanted to work tirelessly to propagate the message of Sai Baba -- do good to others and good will come to you. I sincerely believe that we must do something urgently to bring people from different faiths closer to one another."

Seventy per cent of the movie has already been shot in Delhi, Mumbai and Vrindavan. It is being directed by Faisal Saif and stars besides Aushim in the lead role, Pakistani actor Meera, who is playing a media person from the neighbouring country. Milind Gunaji, Kiran Kumar and Prem Sapru are other actors in this film. Aushim has also come out with a comic adapted from his earlier film Shirdi Sai Baba . Published by the Shirdi Sai Baba Foundation, the comic revolves around key sequences and incidents from Baba's life which were shown in the movie. "After making its first celluloid appearance a decade back, the theme of Shirdi Sai Baba's life and times is all set to capture the print market."

Noting that the film on Sai Baba was recognised at the national level, Aushim says it won the National Integration award. "We have received an overwhelming response from Sai devotees. Over 20,000 comics have already sold out and we hope and pray that millions of children, youth and adults across the world get hold of these comics so that they can understand the message of Sai Baba."

Cricket controversy in the newspapers

Actual scenes from Om Allah

President K. R. Naryanan giving award for National Integration (2002) at the President house

Honoured by Faridabad Sai Samaj

Sai Ki Mahima show at Vrindavan for old age people

Shooting of Om Allah at Kusum Sarovar in Goverdhan

Praying before Baba

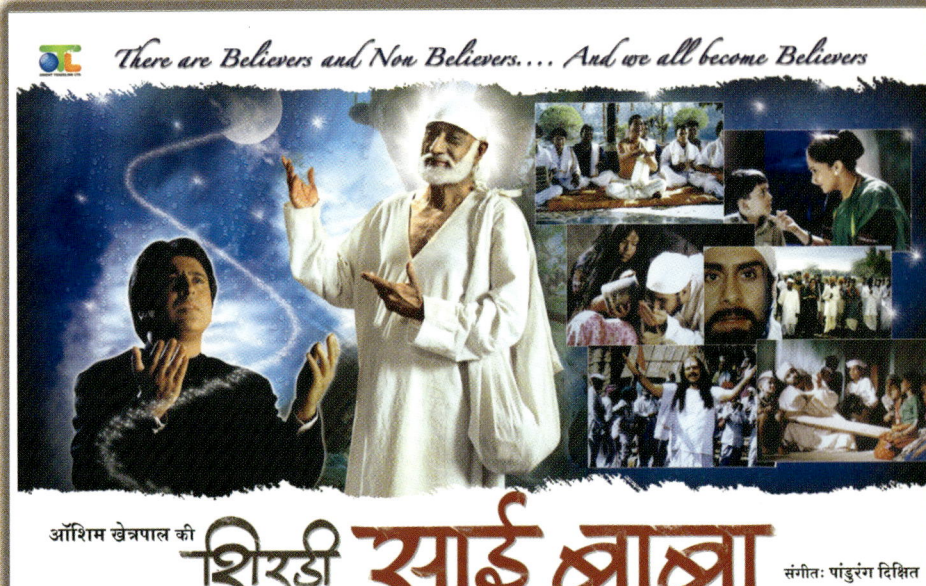

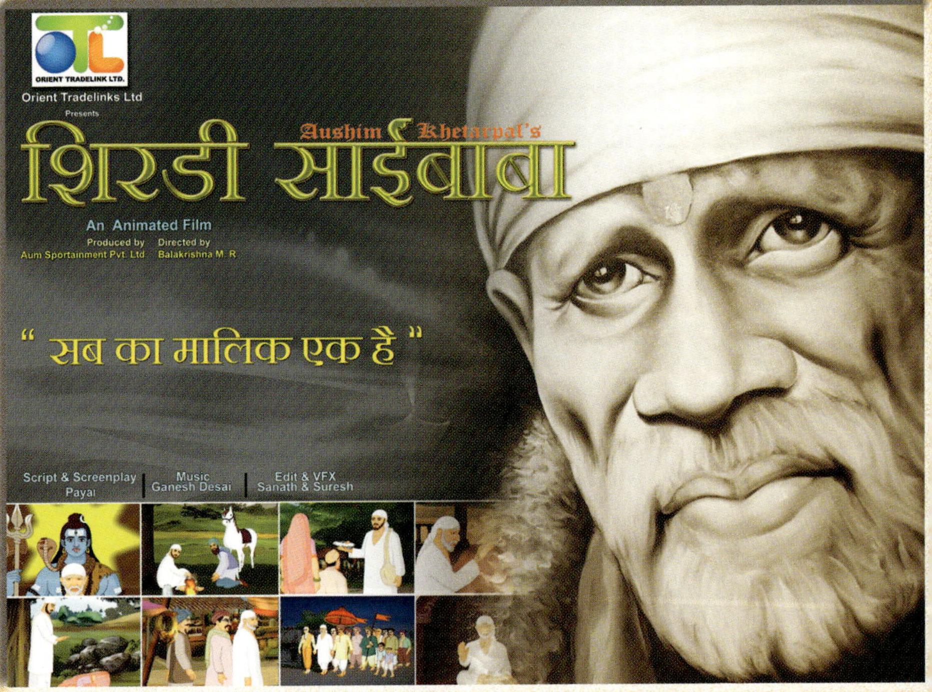

Animated film Shirdi Sai Baba produced by SSBF

Head Priest Sh. Vivek Giri of Sai Dham Mandir Vrindavan with temple devotees

Pradeep Mathur MLA, Mathura at the Bhoomi Poojan of the Sai Mandir at Vrindavan

Sai Ki Mahima TV Show

Neena Arora (sister) getting president award for best screen play for film Page 3

He was in a state of shock. His company had to be shut off and he lost everything. All his properties got attached. Earlier on he had to face personal losses but this was too big a professional loss. Little did he know that the Divine had something else in store for him. There were too many creditors and he had nowhere way to go.

Here his wife's faith in Sai Baba helped him. She told him about Baba and his miracles. At this time she was planning her trip with kids and her parents to Shirdi. Aushim decided to join them at the last moment.

8

Something was going to change now

It is said when Divine intervention takes place, everything changes, and usually it is believed that it changes for good. People find improvements in their situations; their problems just vanish and it becomes a smooth ride from then on.

But invariably, the relationship with the Divine also has a honeymoon period, where one experiences HIS full force, watch miracles happen, pain vanishing and new doors of hope opening. For some time it remains a smooth ride but from then the tests start and one feels that it is the Divine who is testing. But, it is very important for us to understand why would God test us and that too so rigorously? No, instead, it is our deep rooted *sanskaars*, habits, belief systems and subconscious which become roadblocks to the path of growth- -professional, personal and spiritual. On the other another belief so strongly embedded in our subconscious mind is HE is directing everything; whatever I do or happen is God's will. This is a question we all need to ask ourselves. For example, as a parent, when our child does anything wrong, whose will is that? Ours or the child's?

And, even if we want, can we do anything to prevent the punishment? At most, we can give unconditional love and acceptance for the child to heal fast.

Same is the case with our relationship with GOD. HE IS OUR PARENT, and as a parent HE gives us the free will to create and HE is there to teach us and guide us to be on a path which will lead us to the purpose of our life. But we decide to experiment and with our free will create our own world. Sometimes we succeed and create something new but sometime we fail and get hurt. And, this is the time when we seek advice from our parent, GOD, for the right path. It is important that we submit completely for His advice as we would have done with our biological parents. This Divine parent, ocean of unconditional love and forgiveness, first heals us and then shows us the right path.

Again it is our own free will to either walk on the path shown by Him or let the vices take over.

But if you are the CHOSEN ONE, your path is little different because of the kind of work being bestowed on you. This is the time when one has to be really careful and prepared. One must realize the importance of oneself to whom Divine has chosen to reveal HIMSELF and has the faith in him to do the work designated by HIM. But, invariably one fails, as nobody has ever taught us the ways of the Divine and we only see it as they come to us.

Intervention of Divine in one's life allows one to move above the three dimensional existence of the humans to the fourth and fifth dimensions of existence when we change from *human beings having a divine experience* to *divine beings having a human experience*. The real journey starts from HERE!

For Aushim also, it started this way.

He started with his family for Shirdi and with great difficulty reached a place near it. They didn't have money to go further. He just closed his eyes and suddenly he saw Baba calling him. He heard Baba saying, 'So finally you have come! You are my son. Now go and do my prachar, people need it,' and then he vanished.

Aushim opened his eyes.

The experience was too real and vivid in his mind.

And MIRACLES STARTED HAPPENING.

Suddenly there came a car, calling if somebody wanted to go to Shirdi as the car was going there. The car fellow didn't charge them. Till date Aushim thinks it was Baba who had come to help them.

They reached Shirdi.

Sitting below the *neem* tree Aushim prayed to Baba, 'I have lost everything, now you take care of my kids and family and let me move on. I want to give up my life because I can't go on like this.'

Once again he heard His ethereal, loving voice, 'You are my son, just do my prachar, nothing else. I'll take care of everything else.'

Aushim thought about it but couldn't understand the nuances of Baba's message. At night, instinctively he called some of his promoters in Mumbai-- lo and behold, the miracles had started.

They had heard about his problems and wanted to help him out. They were ready to put in money for some of his projects.

Then he called another acquaintance who owed him some money; surprisingly, he was ready to send him the money that day itself, and suddenly he saw money coming from different quarters.

This time money came in hoards and so did the opportunities.

His faith in Baba increased.

Unfortunately, we in India, the land of spirituality, have only understood God as the one who can change everything and solve all problems of our life.

We pray, give penance, ask for forgiveness for all the sins, known or unknown, done by us without even realizing what a sin is.

For Aushim as well, as the money started flowing, his faith in Sai Baba increased.

He felt Baba was happy with him and now there'll be no problem in his life.

But the past experiences had left many wounds which needed to be healed.

The burning desire to be famous was still there.

While working with the celebrities and sports stars he had understood that as their promoter he'll always have to depend on their whims and fancies.

From his last experience, when almost everything he owned was lost, he remembered no one had come forward to his help.

He had learnt his lesson that he is completely alone in this world and has to work for himself.

After visiting Shirdi, strange things started happening in his life. Till then Aushim was writing his own destiny. He had created his own life, made his own plans, worked on them and saw the results; but now he was no more the master of his own life.

It was as if someone else was writing his destiny. A man who is used to plan his way, it was frustrating to see his plans failing but as he was quick to adapt and change, he would look for another deal, another plan.

Gradually, he realized whenever he did something with his projects like organizing an event or any other work, it would fail; but whenever he thought of doing something for Baba, it worked.

It happened again when he planned making a film on Sai Baba. It was just a miracle. He didn't know from where the money will come as none of his businesses were doing well. His wife was very unhappy with him. She felt he was wrong at every step and blamed him to be conceited and arrogant.

He himself was very confused at what was happening in his life.

At one point he was connecting with Baba; the clairvoyance which he had earlier was becoming stronger.

On the other hand all his ventures were failing; he was losing in all his businesses.

This was the beginning of the transformation from a normal, ordinary man to GOD's man.

He needed money for different works he was engaged in. He had to meet many financiers for the money he needed and sometimes they were not the right kind of people.

Another twist in this tale of Divine and his instrument took place during this time.

It is said, when divine enters your life, the devil within you surfaces and attacks you with full force and that was exactly what happened with Aushim.

Aushim was passionate about sports, especially cricket. Whenever he would be watching a match on TV he would predict the scores or the outcomes of the game. It was a sort of childhood passion to predict the result.

It was April 1998.

Once he was sitting with an acquaintance in a restaurant and a cricket match was going on. Aushim predicted the outcome of the match with exact precision and went home.

Next day, he received a lakh of rupees at home. His servant took the packet when no one was at home. When Aushim saw the money and name of the sender he was taken aback. He called up the man and asked about this money. The man replied with pride that as he is an honest man, and on Aushim's prediction he had put a bet which obviously he had won, this money was Aushim's share. Aushim was flabbergasted and shouted at the cheekiness of the man but the man pacified him and requested him to take the money as a gift and not as a share.

Aushim was in dire need of the money and therefore haltingly accepted it.

He thought it is not him who is betting so he cannot be responsible. Now this guy started taking tips from him off and on about the outcomes of different matches. For Aushim once again it was a proof that he was special. He enjoyed the power he felt by making these predictions. Most of Aushim's predictions proved to be true.

It was easy money and a lot of it. It continued for a year.

Other than the money it was his ego which got the biggest boost in this whole process. His wife kept on warning him. She was not happy with these incidences. Having a deep understanding of *karma* philosophy, she cautioned Aushim about the repercussions of using clairvoyance, a divine gift, for betting. Aushim would listen to her, accept it, decide to get out of it but again would get into the web.

Her fears were not unfounded.

9

Controversy

IT WAS JUNE 1999.

The previous year he had organized Salmaan–Karishma Kapoor Nite in the benefit of Punjab Cricket Association which was a huge success and PCA was able to raise lot of money through that event.

Aushim was gaining his confidence again. He was getting into films. Money was flowing in. It was June 1999. He decided to make a film on 'Kargil' as it was the hot and fresh topic in people's mind. Things were getting finalized; on the other hand his love for cricket had started pulling him towards it.

Aushim's relationship with PCA chief revived and he was offered to organize a benefit match between India and Sri Lanka. Aushim deposited a 15-lakh Bank Guarantee to PCA for this match which was to be held in July 1999. But once again destiny had something else in store for him. The animosity between the PCA chief, Mr. I.S. Bindra and BCCI chief, Mr. Jagmohan Dalmiya played heavily for Aushim.

He had to pay a big price for this. The BCCI Chief didn't allow Sri Lanka to come to India to play the match. The match couldn't take place and Aushim lost about one crore in this deal.

More than the money it was his reputation which was at stake.

In late August that same year, he went to London, where England-New Zealand match was taking place. Aushim wanted to revive PCA's offer and met New Zealand's captain, Stephen Flemings to invite him to play in that benefit match. During that meeting, in Fleming's hotel room, Aushim and Fleming were watching United Manchester match and started talking about match-fixing. Watching the match and seeing United Manchester losing Fleming said, 'this match is fixed.' Then he started talking about matches getting fixed. He confessed that they (New Zealand) had once deliberately lost to Zimbabwe, so that they will not have to face Australia in the finals. Aushim offered him and his team a fee of 80,000 pounds to play in the benefit match which was decided by PCA. Fleming refused and Aushim left after leaving his visiting card. During his stay in London, as Aushim was searching for a team, a grocery store owner, Mr. Patel took him to meet Chris Lewis of England's team. Aushim asked him to be a conduit for his team to play in the benefit match. Lewis agreed and said that he'll talk to the manager regarding the match. Aushim left leaving his business card and the company's letter head, so that they could sign the contract if the team or the manager agrees. However, Chris Lewis later refused to play the match.

Crest fallen Aushim returned to India on 31st August.

He now decided that he will concentrate on films. 3rd September was his film's director, Deepak Balraj's birthday. He had come home to discuss the script of the film. He experienced a miracle at Aushim's place. There was *vibhuti* coming from Baba's picture. Deepak was awed at this but for Aushim and his family it was a common phenomenon. Deepak was surprised, 'why haven't you told the world about this? It's the biggest miracle after the milk drinking story of Lord Ganesha.'

Aushim said, 'my wife thinks it's a blessing and protection from Baba and do not want it to be known to the world.'

Putting the Vibhuti on her daughter's forehead Aushim said, 'usually it is Vibhuti but sometimes there's honey which comes from Baba's Pratima's feet and sometimes we find roti and rice. We usually collect them and use them in the daily puja.

Deepak's mouth fell open, 'you are really blessed, Aushim. Why don't we make a film on this miracle!'

Though the discussion ended there, later, Aushim started exploring the idea of making a film on Baba's life. Never to let go any innovative, interesting and profitable idea Aushim was quick to take his decisions and even quicker in implementing them. This quickness and alertness of his mind and then timely implementation had saved him many times. In fact with him it always looked like an order from above, because, once the decision has been taken it was very rare that he would go back on his word. Aushim picked up on Deepak's suggestion and decided to make a film on Life of Baba. Once the decision was made, Aushim took no time to take action. Script was being finalized, casting was being done, and by 10th September they recorded the first song of the film. Meanwhile PCA secretary asked Aushim to once again approach Sri Lanka team so that the benefit match could be revived. Aushim flew to Sri Lanka to talk to the team manager. While he was in Colombo, the biggest blow of his life was erupting in Calcutta.

It is said that Destiny child's life has many milestones, but one life changing experience. Aushim experienced this in September 1999.

A story in a newspaper from Kolkata started doing the rounds that Aushim has offered a bribe of Rs. 3 Crore to Chris Lewis for losing a match.

Within days, it was headlines in all the newspapers.

Everyone was writing what they could about Aushim.

This was just the tip of an iceberg.

It was the first time Indian media had learnt the art of taking mileage out of controversies. All sorts of stories started doing the rounds about Aushim.

Aushim was dumbstruck. He didn't know how to react. Such a huge controversy snowballed out of his casual conversation with Fleming.

Aushim fought back. But to his surprise, his own buddies, including Mr. Bindra or Mr. Dalmiya, refused to help him. He was left alone in this controversy. Press was writing and digging all stories about Aushim. Anita and children were left to comprehend what was happening. Their life was at a standstill.

There were TV Channels, media people and general public waiting in front of his house.

Another blow came towards him, when Fleming accused him for bribing.

It was a very taxing and strange time of his life, he felt everything was slipping through his hands; nothing he said or did made sense. It was as if the whole World was against him. Every day someone or the other would make some allegation against him and it would be the bold headline. His life was being ripped in print and TV. Every work he had achieved was seen as fraud or fabricated. Press was out to get him. He who was the blue eyed sports promoter and most sought after entrepreneur had suddenly turned into this loud mouth middle man who was selfish and completely self centered man without any ethics.

MATCH-FIXING

The Quick-Fix Agent by Aniruddha Bahal

HE used to get his own pictures published in Indian newspapers eulogising himself as an up-and-coming film star. He's held press conferences announcing he's getting Bjorn Borg and Jimmy Connors to play in India. Last week, according to London tabloid

News of the World , it was him, Aushim Khetarpal, proprietor of Radiant Sports Management, who made an offer of £300,000 to former English cricketer Chris Lewis to persuade English players Alec Stewart and Allan Mullaly to throw a Test match against New Zealand in August.

Lewis was apparently asked by Khetarpal to offer similar sums to wicketkeeper-batsman Stewart and fast bowler

Mullaly for dropping catches and bowling wides respectively. Lewis's encounter with Khetrapal took place in the shop of West London newsagent Kamlesh Patel. Says Lewis, who has been a long-time acquaintance of the Patels, "I was introduced to people who offered what they called a business proposal—but it was a bribe wrapped up as a business proposition. If they are offering £300,000 at the bottom of the chain then there must be an awful lot more money involved in it." After the effort to bribe Lewis failed, Khetrapal is reported to have directly approached New Zealand captain Stephen Fleming on the eve of the Test match. Later, Fleming, supposedly, identified Khetrapal to the authorities. Say sources familiar with the incidents, "Khetrapal might just be the tip of the iceberg. The investigations might dig up a lot of dirt."

Outlook managed to trace Khetrapal in Sri Lanka where he's currently scouting for locales for his music video. Says he, "I have worked with people like Vijay Amritraj, Rohit Bal and Jansher Khan. I'm aghast at these charges. I deny the charges by Lewis and Fleming. I talked to and met Fleming but it was basically about representing him for newspaper columns and some television work when he arrives for the New Zealand series in India. I went through Kamlesh Patel, who was referred to me by film producer Jagdish (of Hum Dil De Chuke Sanam fame), as a friend of Lewis and someone who might be able to help me get an English team for a benefit match I was organising in Mohali for the Punjab Cricket Association secretary M.P. Pandove. When I met Lewis there were six other people there. There was a bit of haggling over the money to be paid to the English players. I was willing to pay anything from £70,000 to £90,000. Lewis said it would be difficult to get Stewart and Darren Gough. I told him to get at least eight current Test players. The match got cancelled because of Indian board politics. I'm suing both News of the World and Lewis. I have got Lewis's mobile number in his own handwriting with me. Lewis even called me at my Holiday Inn hotel. Personally, I have got into various controversies but this tops them all. Somebody is telling me now that Lewis has drug problems and sold his story to the paper."

In the book 'Not Quite Cricket' by Indian Express journalist Pradeep Magazine, Khetrapal boasts of how he got the academy going. Says he, "I approached a business house and told them that I need finances for starting an academy at the Modern School tennis courts. They agreed. My next step was to approach the Modern School authorities and tell them that a big business house was ready to finance a tennis academy and it would be good publicity for the school. They agreed too. Thus started the Radiant Tennis Academy. Luckily for me, a son of the director-general of Doordarshan was in the academy. I came very close to this man. He became like my godfather. I tied up with Four Square to organise the national championship and made arrangements with Doordarshan to show it live. That was the first time a sports meet was shown live on television. That's why I say I'm the man who started it all."

ONE of the former students at the academy, however, has this to say about Khetrapal, "I was doing well. Winning local tournaments etc." But he was very passionate about his students at the Radiant Tennis Academy Says a senior journalist who knows Khetrapal well, "A favourite quote of his used to be 'I can try selling kabbadi to corporate sponsers and I think I will be successful." In pre-satellite channel days he once convinced Videocon to sponsor the Asia Cup in cricket.

He sold them the idea by saying that the President would come to inaugurate the tournament. Of course, that never happened. Videocon rarely stepped into cricket sponsorship after that. Magazine has devoted nearly four pages to Khetrapal and calls him a self-styled sports promoter who claims to have made a valuable contribution to cricket. Khetrapal himself makes tall claims about his company. Magazine quotes him as saying that he has signed on Pakistani cricketers Wasim Akram and Saqlain Mushtaq. There's also something of the narcissistic streak in him.

Incidentally, Khetrapal was in London during the World Cup and tried to bid for the quadrangular tournament currently on in Kenya. He was, apparently, trying to make a comeback after he ran into trouble with income tax authorities who had raided his house and slapped him with a tax evasion case worth Rs 4 crore. Other deals brokered by him in the past include getting Jansher Khan, the Pakistani squash champion, to play in the Mahindra tournament in Mumbai. He approached him through Zaheer Abbas. Lately, Khetrapal has been more involved in veterans cricket. Says a player who has played in one of the Khetrapal-organised series, "These matches are fishy." In the recent Lewis-Fleming operation, Khetrapal even left his visiting card with the players. In Fleming's case he checked into the New Zealand team hotel in Leicester along with another Indian businessman. The New Zealand captain, of course, immediately reported the approach to the International Cricket Council. Scotland Yard is now investigating the two offers and police officers might be coming to India to question Khetrapal.

The caveat is, of course, Khetrapal's opinion on betting in cricket, as delivered to Magazine. Says he, "It is only when big betting comes to a sport that it becomes big. The only thing wrong here is that players are throwing away matches. They should not sell the nation. Otherwise, betting will generate a lot of money for the game. It is not a bad thing. It will do more good than harm." Well, interesting.

V.K. SANTOSH KUMAR OCTOBER 18, 1999

The big fix

Latest charges of match-rigging give ICC chance to decide on strict action

Cricket, it is said, is in a mess. It is tough to argue. Match-fixing, for instance, is a virus eating fast into the fabric of cricket. But the game's administrators have preferred to close their eyes, praying that it will miraculously go away.

When the Australian Cricket Board realised Shane Warne and Mark Waugh were guilty of accepting $11,000 (Rs.4.73 lakh) from an Indian bookie, both it and David Richards of the International Cricket Committee (ICC) decided, inexplicably, to keep it a secret.

Promises to keep: Jagmohan Dalmiya aims to rid the game of undesirable elements.

When Justice Y.V. Chandrachud conducted, by many accounts, a facile investigation into match-fixing in India, the ICC preferred to turn a blind eye. More recently when the Pakistan Cricket Board suspended its captain Wasim Akram and then reinstated him, no one raised an eyebrow.

Amazingly, despite a new story every month - like Indian sports promoter Aushim Khetarpal allegedly offering 300,000 pounds (Rs.2.1 crore) each to England cricketer Chris Lewis and New Zealand captain Stephen Fleming to tank a match - not one cricketer has been evicted from the game or anyone sued for slander.

"We are not Nazis. We can't be dictatorial," says Jagmohan Dalmiya, president of the ICC. In a sense he's right, for match-fixing is the responsibility of the board concerned. As Tony Greig says, "It's going to take an individual board to bite the bullet, prosecute someone and then drive him out of the game." Yet with the boards reluctant to indict players, the ICC needs to set the standard. Says Bishan Bedi: "Match-fixing is getting global.

As caretakers of a great institution, the ICC should own up responsibility." In that context, the ICC's decision to set up a three-member Code of Conduct Commission to look into all aspects of match-fixing, though belated, is a welcome move.

The central figures: Aushim Khetarpal

Headed by Lord Hugh Griffiths, former MCC president and judge, and assisted by Sir Oliver Popplewell, retired British high court judge, and Albie Sachs, judge in the constitutional court of South Africa, the commission will meet in London from the third week of October to chart a course of action.

On its priority list, interestingly, is reopening the Indian and Australian reports. "The board reports are not binding on the ICC, if they are inadequate the ICC will investigate on its own," says Dalmiya. "I'm telling the member countries, before the game is played for bookies, let's swing into action." To display his determination, Dalmiya explains that he has also asked the Pakistan board to send its report to the ICC immediately.

Who will carry out the investigation, however, constitutes a problem. As Greig says, "You've got to have the arm of the law involved." It is admirable therefore that when Lewis accused Khetarpal, the England and Wales Cricket Board immediately referred the matter to Scotland Yard. A spokesman for the Yard confirmed that an "investigation by the Metropolitan Police Service's organised crime group is ongoing".

As usual, in this case it is one man's word against the other. Lewis, in and out of the English team, spilled his story to *News of the World* fuelling suspicions that he was paid a "six-figure sum". James Millbank, the author of the piece, though is vehement that the player has not been paid a penny. Khetarpal is no angel either.

A sports promoter who branched off into managing individual players, syndicating columns, organising celebrity events and producing television programmes, he has a rather unsavoury reputation.

Billiards ace Michael Ferreira, for one, started collaborating with him in the early 90s but the partnership soured after a few years. "He started off as a sound sports promoter but his interest in sports finised after the controversy. He was very passionate about his country," says Ferreira.

Khetarpal who claims his company Radiant Sports Management, had a turnover of Rs.9 crore last year, says, "If I had Rs.7 crore to pay these players, I would rather have spent it on an event. After 10 years in the sports promotion business this is the most ridiculous thing to get into. It stinks."

His version is that he never approached Lewis to fix a match. He was only trying to put together an England XI to play a benefit match against an Indian XI (to be coordinated by Ajay Jadeja) at Mohali in September under the aegis of the Punjab Cricket Association.

Lewis, on the contrary, claims he was approached by Khetarpal at newsagent Kamlesh Patel's house in West London to fix an England-New Zealand match during the recent series. "I was introduced to some people who said they had a business proposal," said Lewis to *News of the World*. "But it was a bribe wrapped as a business proposition."

The central figures: Chris Lewis   *The central figures: Stephen Fleming*

On the ICC's priority list is reopening the Indian and Australian reports.

The stories, however, don't seem to tally completely Khetarpal admits he met Lewis and the captains of New Zealand and " West Indies, Stephen Fleming and Brian Lara, in England between July 29 and August 2 to get them to play in Mohali.

He says he met Fleming for breakfast at the Holiday Inn in Leicester and even presented him a watch and his mother a shawl. However, John Reid, former Test player and operations manager, New Zealand board, told INDIA TODAY that in Fleming's report he only mentions that he was approached by "someone" at the hotel's foyer. **There's no mention of Khetarpal by name - even though the sports promoter says he left his business card with Fleming - or about any money being offered.**

Khetarpal promises to sue the *News of the World* for 1 pound million (Rs.7 crore), says, "My conscience is clear. I'm ready to face any enquiry." The ICC needs to take him at his word and ensure a detailed investigation is carried out. If Lewis is lying he should be dismissed from the game; if Khetarpal is guilty he should pay a heavy penalty. The bottom line is: after years of loose talk, it's time for some action.

It pained Aushim to see his name being tarnished like this and most hurting was that his near and dear ones from media and also personal friends were talking against him.

He kept his head high. Every day in the morning there'll be a long chain of reporters in front of his house with another new allegation creating hurt and pain in this proud man, but he would keep the aggression on so that he'll not buckle down but the pain was too deep which came out in the form of retaliation.

1 OCT 25, 1999

Fiction of the Fact

It's a beautiful morning as I sit down to react to your story on me (The Quick-Fix Agent, October 11). I can hear birds chirping on trees across the lane, my wife's voice in the next room urging my two little daughters to get dressed. If you meet my wife, and ask about me you'd see a spark in her eyes. I ask you, Mr Editor, what was on your mind when you cleared the story? Your reporter could only find people who had bad things to say about me. Allow me to point out the Ôfiction' in the report:

a) A journalist who says I can make a fool of a person 64 times. Who's he?;

b) Like there are many hotels in Delhi where I didn't end up paying bills. Where are these hotels?;

c) Steffi Graf couldn't come to India because Babri Masjid happened in '92 and there was a sense of fear and insecurity all around;

d) Like Videocon. They were the ones who were asked by the court to pay the money they were defaulting just a day before the Asian Cup;

e) I am said to be narcissistic. Is informing people about my film narcissistic?;

f) As for the Rs 4 crore tax evasion report, I fought the case and won it;

g) My veterans matches 'are fishy'. Why're they so? What's fishy when national selectors like Madan Lal and Ashok Malhotra play in them?;

h) A book is quoted as saying I am for betting. It is not betting, but match-fixing which is evil.

Aushim Khetrapal Radiant Sports Management

The pain and hatred was becoming unbearable but on the other hand press, although was against him but kept printing his versions and retaliations as well. Eventually, the story died down but his whole life had changed. Whatever name he had earned in these years was suddenly in circle of mistrust. On the face of it all the friends and relatives shared their sympathy but in their eyes he could feel doubts, antagonism and resentment.

Aushim retaliated in the press by announcing that Chris Lewis was a drug addict. He was flabbergasted at the turn of the events. But press stood by Aushim and kept on writing his versions as well.

For ten days the story remained alive in press and by 10th October Aushim had proved in press that Chris Lewis had sold his story to News of World for 40,000 pounds.

Aushim filed a clarification suite against News of World and Scotland Yard got involved. However, the story died in press. But something clicked in this young man's heart and he vowed to leave sports and everything associated with it.

In these ten days of tension, pressure and stress the only thing which had kept him going was his will power, his truth and Sai Baba's name.

A saint, Swami Vimlanand, who often visited his home, told him to just write 'Om Sai Ram' to get out of his problem.

Dumb struck with this incidence in his life Aushim asked him, 'why is this happening to me and my family, Swamiji?'

'Remember Aushim, you are the *Arjun* of this *Mahabharat* of cricket. Now all the dirt of this game will go away and you will come out clean. Nothing will happen to you'.

10
Another chapter

Aushim's heart was broken. He announced in his last press conference that he bid good bye to sports and moved over to films.

Shooting of 'Sai Baba' film was also a miracle. There was always a deficit of money. But as if Aushim was compelled to finish the film. Whenever there would be any money, he'll plan the shoot. The trust and confidence he had in the Divine made the film happen; because, from some or the other sources, money always came at the last minute. Aushim also turned to acting and played a major role in the film.

Making of the film on Sai Baba itself required a complete book as the amount of miracles Aushim saw happening during this film were amazing. It was as if some divine power was helping him at each step.

There was a buzz in the industry. People were saying a lot of things about the film. It was already the talk of the town. There were many thoughts and apprehensions doing the rounds in the industry that an outsider has come and made a film on Baba. Generally, most of the producers take their films to Shirdi for Baba's blessings; but it is the 'chosen one' who could make a film on Him. Aushim was being watched with reverence and contempt.

The premier of film saw the whole industry coming to watch the movie, and after the screening was over they had good things to say about the film. But again destiny had another story to write.

September 2011, the week the film got released worldwide, the Twin Towers of New York were attacked by suicide bombers and the world came to a standstill.

The worst affected were the films released during that time. The film didn't make money on the box office. Aushim felt heartbroken; nevertheless he didn't give up. The publicity of the film had already created a stir.

Aushim had lost money on the film but it was the faith of the man in his work and the presence of the Divine, that he never ever, even in the worst scenario of his life, sold the rights of the film. It was his property; his homage to Baba.

Aushim looked, felt and thought about the film with veneration; so much love and trust was attached with this film.

He talked passionately about the film to everyone. It was this man's charm that had a mesmerizing effect. As a soft spoken, well-mannered person, Aushim never showed any aggression in his meetings with people. But it was the enveloping energy of the man which caught the attention of the people around. No one could ever ignore his presence. In fact, mostly it was his absence in their life that made people wary of him.

They could never understand him. He was full of promises and optimism. His passion and gripping energy made people believe in his ideas and thoughts, but the moment he would move away, the uncertainty and fear would come in and hence cause the wariness.

Suddenly, he realized that his reputation was once again stained by controversies. The scandalous cricket betting controversy took away not only his happiness but completely shattered his life, both personally and professionally. There was huge pressure from creditors.

Amidst all these controversies and chaos it was abruptly announced that the Sai Baba Film has been given the President Award for Peace and Harmony.

The constant ups and downs of his life were like a roller coaster ride for him. Every time he thought his life is finished something happened which gave him new hope.

He, with the whole team and family went to Rashtrapati Bhawan to receive the award but still the pains and problems continued.

He was becoming completely disillusioned with his life. Whenever he planned to move one step forward all the forces of the universe would work to take him five steps back. After the award and Scotland Yard giving him a clean chit on controversy involving Fleming, he thought he might be able to lead a peaceful life; but something else was in store for him.

For next few days things were smooth but he was in a hurry. Too much had happened in his life. Too many ups and down he had faced, however, he had confidence in himself that even after every loss he would be able to fight back.

He decided, rather than promoting others he should promote himself. As he was reasonably good looking and always wanted to do films, he thought of making more films. As a sport promoter he had understood one thing that if he can build a brand out of others, he can do it with himself as well. He was a sportsman by heart but acting attracted him more. He learned the nuances of film promotion. He also understood the working of the film industry. Fortunately, he had good relationships with many in the industry. Authority or celebrity statues never bothered him. He started five films simultaneous with big cast. Also, at the same time, he was dabbling in different business. He was also running three Limited Companies and was reaching 350 crore. He was frequently traveling between Delhi and Mumbai. He had six houses, three in Mumbai and three in Delhi – once again he was riding high.

11

The final blow

But, as always, spells of misfortune soon followed him. Suddenly, all his companies had to be closed.

Due to some inconsistency in the dealing of shares all his companies were seized and banned by SEBI. He was down from 350 crore to zero. He has deeply into debt.

He sold off all his properties in a hurry and therefore did not get the market price. He tried paying back all his debts.

He was able to finish off most of it but still 18 crores were left to be paid.

18 crores was not a small amount.

All the works and films on floor had come to ground.

He was in trance. The worst period of his life had started.

It was October 2002. HE WAS 42 AND REMEMBERED GURUJI'S WORDS.

This time it looked everything had stopped.

He thought that as always the way he had moved through all the ups and down, he will be able to find back his way this time as well. So, he agreed to all the debtors' demands. He had faith in himself.

He had seen these ups and downs too many times in his life. As this debacle was quiet a big one, financially, he came in contact with lot of people having dubious backgrounds. There were financiers, who were ready to help him out but with unreasonable rates of interest. Blindly he agreed to everything as he thought, as always, this bad spell will not last for long. He signed all the papers and agreed to all the demands as he didn't have the energy to fight. Also, at the back of his mind, he thought he will come back. As always, he was expecting some miracle to happen and he was quiet sure it'll happen; but with each passing day the situation moved towards worst.

He was trying with all his might but nothing came his way. Pressure was mounting from all sides. People had even started threatening him.

This time even his wife gave up.

Kids were growing up. Facing the creditors every morning was not an easy job. She was becoming fed up. One day she just packed the bags and with kids and moved over to Vrindavan.

Her whole life had also shattered. With two young daughters it was not easy to survive or start the life afresh at some small place; but hats off to the courage of the lady and her believe in Baba-- she started managing their life all alone.

He couldn't stop her because there was nothing he could do. His mother, with whom his relationship had soured over

The final blow

the years had completely given up on him and was with Umang in U.S.

Umang was the only source of courage but he was too far. For the first time in his life he was utterly alone; completely, absolutely alone. It was as if the Divine powers, the hold he had over objects or things was also not with him. He had lost his face among the creditors. They were using all sorts of techniques to slaughter him. But he fought back.

He didn't have any place to live, no money to even eat and as he never had any friend he had no one to turn to.

Aushim didn't know which way to go or which business to start. All his aspirations, desires and projects were at stand still. Nothing was moving, Whenever he'll take a step further, he felt he was being taken two steps back. When the film got the national integration award, rumors were that it was rigged. The time was such that whatever he did was taken with a pinch of mistrust and doubt. He was doing his best to make his projects work; there were still many takers who would get under his spell and were ready to go with him. Also there were people who felt he is a nice, good man but couldn't make out what was wrong with his life or what were the mistakes he was making that resulted in his miseries.

All his friends, colleagues and relatives felt that he chews more than he can digest and that's why he had to face the failures. To them he was too ambitious for his own good but the thing that they did not realize was that for Aushim it was his only survival aid. He never gave up; even at his lowest, he kept his spirits up which at times hovered to arrogance but he had to do it. Everyday, in the morning, he'll get up and give himself the boost of confidence that he is the best.

Another amazing fact he realized about human beings and their emotions is that once a person has gone down, everyone wants to see him crying, miserable and broken. Then only they feel the person deserves their sympathy and help. But when they see the person who has gone through so much is still standing high and not crouching down, they can't take it.

Aushim was shocked to find his near and dear ones making comments such as 'he is still not learning, still lives in a fool's paradise and he will again fall back'. He was amazed at the human psychology of putting a person down when that person is already so low, instead of appreciating his efforts to revive himself. He felt completely alone and the hatred and anger of his own people made him even sad. For the first time in his life, he wanted to give up. He, who was the epitome of life force, who was always able to find an opening in the darkest of circumstances, had reached the darkest point of his life. And then he fell ill. Seriously ill.

12

The Divine and the bhakt

Amidst all these, for the first time in his life, he fell sick. He had a major stomach problem and had to be admitted in a hospital for a month. He was almost on his death bed. No one was with him. In such utter desperation and loneliness, he called Baba, "you had called me your son. Where did I go wrong? Why has such misfortune befallen on me?" He heard an ethereal voice say, "this, my son, is the end of the suffering; the last misfortune. This one is the most devastating misfortune of all. You will lose everything. But son, you must remember, only the one who has lost all, can conquer the world."

Aushim cried like a child-- a lonely, helpless and broken child. Baba said, 'Son, you are my real bhakt. You cannot be tired. You have to become detached from all your attachments. You have the responsibility of giving the world my knowledge. You may feel that this is too huge a responsibility, but let me tell you one thing. I have my hand on your head. I will give you the powers and strength to face the world and to carry out this duty."

"But why do I have this responsibility? Why can't I have a normal ordinary life? Why do I have to walk on this path alone? Why me?"

"Because this is your Karma. You are destined for this."

Finally Aushim got some peace. He composed himself and decided to actually set on the path to fulfill his *dharma*, his most important duty.

Aushim went into a deep sleep. He had no idea for how long he was asleep, but when he woke up, many doctors were gathered around him, staring wide eyed, as if they had seen a living ghost. Wondering what the reason was for their awkwardness, Aushim asked a patient in the nearby room about what had happened to Aushim, pretending to be someone else. He found out that the usually quiet and arrogant Aushim was talking to someone. Initially, the doctors thought that he was talking to the nurse standing nearby. Later, they realized that he was actually talking to somebody invisible! Aushim was shocked and embarrassed. Doubts crept into his already dazed mind, "was all that just a dream? Just my imagination?" After a while, he decided to listen to his heart. His heart was confident that Baba had visited him.

There was miraculous healing to his sickness. Doctors were amazed at his tremendous will power. He was feeling much better. In the evening, one of his old friends called up, who owed him around 2 lakhs. He had heard about Aushim's financial crisis and wanted to return the money. Aushim was ecstatic. Something had changed. Although the situations, the people and the hatred were still the same, Aushim had changed.

His will power had returned and also his confidence; but this time there was no wariness towards people. He felt differently towards them. Till now, he was at odds with them, either he ignored them or talked to them when needed. Actually, till now, he had not noticed people with empathy in his heart; either he was fighting them or appeasing them. Now he could look at them and feel a wave of love towards them. It was not natural. His own people had always said that he was not a 'people's people' and now he realized that he had never noticed people as individual identities. They were there, that's all. But now, he started noticing them. In the hospital itself his attitude towards nurses and doctors became different. One night when a nurse came to give him his medicine, he just told her, 'do not worry about you mother. She will be diagnosed correctly this week. It will be tuberculosis. But with proper medication she will be fine.' The nurse was shocked and so was he.

He did not know why he was saying that but the lady started crying. She told him the whole story-- how her mother has been unwell for three months and doctors were not able to diagnose her problem. The whole family had been worried about her. Then she asked him how he knew it and he said he just knew it. Then he gave her Baba's photo which was with him.

Aushim was amazed at himself. He didn't know what he was doing. It was as if someone was compelling him to tell people what to do and how to come out of their miseries. But he was still in thick of his own mess.

Another change which was now taking place in him was the assurance of Sai Baba at his side. Till now he had been uncertain about this Divine presence but now he felt the constant company of Sai Baba. Even if there was nobody in his life, he was still fighting the battles. The conversation with Baba was constant source of inspiration to move on and do things.

Life was moving on.

Aushim had more than 200 court cases to be sorted out. His family was not with him and he was all alone. Still there was a confidence in him. He would have these conversations with Baba in his semi-sleep state. Baba would tell him what to do next. Next two years, it was as if Aushim was in trance. He would exactly do what Baba would say. And things started happening in his favor.

A thorough marketing man by nature, Aushim knew the power of media. Even if Sai Baba film had not done well in the box office it was shown on television. The satellite rights of the film were with Star TV and it was shown almost every Saturday. On the other hand, cable channels started showing it every Thursday.

As it was destined in the worlds time cycle, Shirdi Sai Baba became a household name in North India and so did Aushim's face. People on the road would stop him and recognize him as Baba's follower. They would point out at him and say, 'Sai Baba'. Aushim would just smile but he was amazed at this sudden turn of events. Suddenly on one hand were his creditors and on the other the Sai devotees or his fans.

People started telling him about the miracles of Baba they were experiencing in their life. Meeting veteran writer and Sai Bhakt, Vikas Kapoor was another turning point of his life. He spent most grueling and difficult but also learning times with Kapoor. They'll have long discussions on religion, power of the religion, importance of religiousness and God

The Divine and the bhakt

in one's life. These discussions made him aware of his own spirituality and understanding.

Based on the true stories of devotees of Sai Baba, Aushim started a TV Series, 'Sai Bhakton Ki Sachchi Kahaniyan' on Sony TV. He had a sponsor for the series but as usual it didn't work out and Aushim lost lots of money.

On the other hand the series became a hit and people got attached to it. By hook or crook Aushim kept the series alive on some channel or the other. One more thing he realized that for some reason Baba didn't want anyone else to put in money and that was why people were not coming up with usual business proposals. Aushim was realizing that his other businesses were coming to a standstill. He needed money to pay back his debts and make projects for spreading Baba's message.

In August, 2007 he opened the Shirdi Sai Baba Foundation. A family man by nature, he created a Divine Family: Sai Bhakt Parivaar. The foundation opened for membership and people willingly started getting attached to it.

By now Aushim had given up all his aspirations and dedicated his entire time to Baba. Another milestone in the Foundation and Aushim's life was round the corner.

This was strange and 'never heard of' era in TV. Globally, it was in the time when concept of religion and spirituality had to be redefined and had to become available to the common being. Suddenly with few players, religion and spirituality was coming out of the closed doors of ashrams, maths and religious places to people's drawing rooms through satellite television. Till now TV channels would pay the producers for creating TV programmes and then generate revenue by getting advertisements and sponsors from different brands, but a very new brand of revenue stream was just waiting for the religious TV channels. Around this time the rich and wealthy disciples of these Sanyasis and Babas came forward to pay the channels huge amount of money to telecast the *katha* or the *satsang* of their gurus. It was a complete revolution. Because of technological marvel, the common man sitting in a small town can see and listen to a *Ram katha* or *pravachan* taking place in Vrindavan. Spirituality and religion was reaching people's household at their convenience. This was a major shift. Elders at home felt thrilled and kids and youngster also got a taste of their religion and heritage. But, on the other hand, there came a horde of *satgurus* and astrologers who paid huge amount of money to get time slots in order to make huge amount of money using this medium. Their modus operandi was to create fear and uncertainty in the viewers' mind. Suddenly everyone wanted to know about their future. These ancient Indian sciences, whose knowledge was kept to few through family and gurukuls was suddenly out in open for everyone to benefit. There was whole new genre of TV programmes based on occult which was attracting Indian audience.

It was the Call of time. Collectively, the sub conscious of the people was searching for these answers. As a whole, society was going through major transition. All the morals and ethics and basic units were breaking down. At one point people's greed was seeing new heights and they were making it their need and on the other hand there were many who had started questioning the existing belief systems related to religion and religious rituals. People were caught in the vicious circle created by their own twisted projections. The financial growth of the middle class had given them the materialistic pleasures and luxuries but had also given the gifts of fear, competition, jealousy and greed. Suddenly, there was a spurt

The Divine and the bhakt

of these new age gurus, who could speak in their language and also could empathize with them, understand their fears and through the help of these sciences could provide them with ritualistic solutions, which created more greed and fear. But, on the whole, this era created awareness about spirituality and religion, which were unquestionable and compartmentalized for ages. People were open to explore for finding the answers to the questions of the mankind.

Aushim had no money to support his ventures and the TV Channels became wary of him. Aushim had another humble beginning with a spiritual channel with a different programme: a chat show named 'Sai Ki Mahima', in which he gave live answers to people's problems through *Sai Satcharitr*.

'Sai Ki Mahima' was a chat show with Aushim Khetarpal in which people got the solutions of their day-to-day problems through Sai Satcharitr. Problems could be as varied as possible -- a relationship problem, health problem, professional or even spiritual problem. People sent their queries by mobile text messages and got answers during the show. Each episode was an interactive session on life's different aspect like stress, values, relationship, profession and many more; and through this spiritual journey the solutions were explored in a practical way interspersed with humor and real-life incidents. Even if the programme was based on spirituality it was very lively, interesting and full of hope and was liked by thousands of viewers worldwide. It became a 'must watch' in their daily routine.

Unexpectedly, the programme became an instant hit with the audiences and phones of the foundation and Aushim's personal phones started ringing continuously. There was an onslaught of people wanting to know about themselves. Some of them wanted to join the foundation. Many of them wanted to meet Aushim with their problems.

Amidst all the gurus, astrologers, healers and preachers on these channels, Aushim was an exception. A cultured, English speaking, soft spoken, smart and good-looking actor talking common sense was a novelty for people. Aushim's life had become a whirl of activities. Doing these live shows in the morning hours, personally taking more than two hundred calls a day, handling the activities of the foundation, handling creditors, generating money for the channels and looking into all cases and attending courts-- at times 24 hours were not enough.

During all these years, as there was no money, a two-room apartment in New Delhi's Sant Nagar was the foundation's office during the day and his shelter at night. Often he would sleep on the floor, eat on the dhabas and travel in autos rickshaws or taxi; but for the first time in his life, Aushim didn't mind.

He didn't even notice this lack of basic luxury. Something inside him was fulfilling. He started praying for others. All the people calling him with their problems became his own. He actually was creating a diverse, big Divine family without even knowing it.

It was as if Divine was actually working through him. On one hand there was this crowd of people who looked up to him as Baba's representative. They would put their complete faith in him. On the other hand there was his past which was catching up. Old acquaintances and colleagues would look at him with suspicion and contempt.

There was an feeling of doubt around him but Aushim's continuous faith and love for Baba kept him going. He was constantly in touch with Sai Bhakts. He himself was amazed at his answers and at times was doubtful about them. But, when people would call back that all his predictions were turning out to be true, he became confident. At times he'll have doubts whether these were his words or Baba's words but soon he was able to discover the truth.

Other than establishing the biggest Divine Sai Bhakt Parivaar, Baba had entrusted him with another mammoth task of creating Giriraj Sai Dham and taking Baba to Krishna Ki Nagri.

Once during his semi-sleep conversation with Baba, he asked him how to raise funds for the temple to be constructed. Baba gave him the idea of 'Brick Donation'. During his lifetime, Baba was very attached to the brick-- he used one a pillow and it was this brick which was mistakenly broken by Ahdul (Baba's confidant) and Baba knew he will have to leave his body.

In his shows, Aushim started propagating 'Eent Daan'. Everyone in the television fraternity ridiculed him and talked behind his back about him selling Baba.

The Sai Prasad which each member received from the Foundation had many merchandise of Baba. This was also ridiculed by many in the industry. But Aushim was not bothered and turned deaf ears to those comments. He only heard ONE VOICE, one sound and that was Baba's!

Gradually people started donating bricks. Each brick was for meager five hundred rupees and the donor will get a gift of Sai Satcharitr and Sai Baba's film DVD.

Within a year more than 50,000 Sai Satchatir's were distributed all over India.

Destiny was writing another script for those devotees who donated bricks. Miracles started happening in their lives. Even Aushim, who was amazed at the turn of the events realized after some time that for the first time in the history a temple will be constructed with the bricks donated by lakhs of people all over the world, and this would be a place of worship truly made by Baba's devotees.

But Aushim's woes had not finished. Building a Sai Dham in the holy city of Vrindavan was not an easy task.

There was rigidity everywhere; Government approvals and permissions were needed to get the roads constructed, and other clearances were to be obtained.

Local villagers were not ready to accept a person from Delhi, a mere outsider to come and takeover, but here also Baba's intervention helped.

At the entrance of Vrindavan, there was a temple which was in shambles and it was the property of the *grampanchayat*. Mahantji was the caretaker who also ran an orphanage for boys and was involved in this noble cause for last two decades.

Aushim was close to Mahantji, both understood the pains, ridicule and constant doubts and uncertainties of being on the path of awareness. Aushim and Mahantji decided to convert that temple into Baba's abode.

It was a difficult and colossal task of creating a huge temple which will have depiction of mythological stories traversed through history and pre-historic epics of Indian gods and goddesses.

There was a legend in the small community of villagers that none of the *Brijwasi* but a short man from outside will come and make a temple there. Mahantji reminded the

The Divine and the bhakt

villagers about this story and Aushim's short physical stature helped in getting the approval of villagers for the required work to start.

In the mean time, the question-answer programme for Sai bhakts was on.

The answers to all their questions came to him of its own. Many of his friends and colleagues suggested that it is a game of probability; when you answer arbitrarily probability of five correct answers out of ten is there.

Aushim also questioned himself: what was he trying to do, how can cleaning of the temple premises get you a job or help you clear your court cases!

He himself was amazed that defying the probability theory nine out of ten answers were correct.

He would come to know about these when people would call up and tell him whatever he had said had happened.

Aushim started praying to Baba for this miracle. He, who was never a people's people suddenly felt responsible towards them and also to their faith in Baba.

Suddenly he realized, it was not he whose reputation was at stake, but Baba's, whom he loved immensely.

In spite of all his weaknesses he possessed one major strength, which was his sense of responsibility, maybe because of his Sunshine that was exalted in Aries in 11th house.

This was also one of reasons of his rigidity and over sensitivity; but over the years even astrologers were baffled at the way his life's incidences were taking place.

Nothing in his natal charts ever indicated the turbulences and ups and downs of such magnitude in his life. But Aushim understood it was someone else chartering the course of his life. He always remembered Baba's words, 'Just hold my hand, continue my work and don't worry about the consequences; no harm will come to you or your family.'

Gradually Aushim realized his family was not just his near and dear ones but a great amount of people who had come close to him because of his programme on question-answers. He realized that through him a real Divine family was being created towards whom he felt responsible.

Another interesting thing he realized about himself that whenever he felt responsible for someone, he cared for that person and vice versa. In other words, whenever he cared for someone, he felt responsible.

By now before he could understand, he had deeply started caring for all the Sai bhakts involved with him in this question-answer programmes. The bhakts, like a family member would call up any time during the day from 5:30 am to 1:30 am. They'll cry, laugh, fret or complain to him about all the problems of their lives and on his part, to be fair to Aushim, he never took offence to these calls and would patiently speak to all of them, and like a true family member advise them and also give Baba's answers. But more than that, it was simple logic and common sense which helped him to answer these people.

At one point, Aushim was taking more than 200 calls a day and surprisingly, still could think rationally. He realized he was enjoying himself; unknowingly he had experienced the secret of life.

To experience unlimited happiness, we need to learn to give **unconditionally** and that's exactly what he was doing. Although he did it as a duty or as Baba's work but what he received was unexplainable: unlimited blessings, love and faith from the Sai bhakt parivaar that healed him.

Aushim realized, he was not angry or remorseful anymore. Earlier he used to say, 'As long as I'll do HIS work, He'll take care of my problems like handling creditors, my projects or my dreams'.

Being a businessman in the true sense, it was a good business deal. He will do HIS work and Prachar, heal HIS people and in return Baba will take care of his works.

But in the process he realized even if his projects were getting delayed, his creditors were still cursing him, he still had no money to live a basic life it didn't matter anymore to him.

Earlier, when his projects would stop, he would stop taking calls, get angry with Baba and go into anger bouts or depression. But now, whatever the situation was, his focus was on question answers, Baba's temple in Vrindavan which had to be constructed and all other projects related to the Foundation.

By now, Aushim was able to set up three call centers to take the incoming and outgoing calls of the bhakts. The Foundation was getting involved in many charitable and social works as well.

A very big Gaushala was being established in Vrindavan.

The foundation had produced an animated film on the life of Sai Baba and Baba Ramsaa Peer in the year 2012-2013 and three more films were in the pipeline.

The foundation has produced first-of-its-kind comic book on Baba, based on the film and also 'Sai Samvad', Sai ki Atamkatha and Sai Satcharitr in poetry written by Urmil

Satya Bhushan which is also based mostly on Aushim's conversations with Baba. The book written by a well-established writer is being appreciated by both bhakts and laureates.

He has completely involved himself in these projects though his associates still have their doubts, people around him are still wary of him but could not avoid him as they know Aushim's ideas and thoughts were much ahead of their vision. TV channels knew he could deliver and therefore could never ignore him.

Being Baba's ambassador he became fearless.

He had accepted his fate: there will always be mistrust, doubt, envy and fear and ultimately acceptance and awe but it no more hurt him.

Because, on the other side there was a huge number of devotees who had complete faith and love for him. His words would solace them, heal them and show them the way.

Aushim was reaching a stage where acceptance of these two diverse emotions had stopped affecting him much.

Nar Singh, present director (coaching), Delhi Lawn Tennis Association (DLTA) which is the state body of the All India Tennis Association (AITA) had been Aushim's tennis partner when they used to play under-14 matches and continued to play together for the college and for Nationals as well tells us, 'Aushim is a great motivator and a winner all through. Every match we played together, his focus was on winning and we were a great team. As a person he is nice, soft spoken and very ambitious. I have known him for last four decades and was with him for few years, and what I like about him is his perseverance and ability to give results, that also very quickly. I was not in touch with him for a long time but last time when we touched base, he talked about Baba and he wanted to do something for Tennis and sports in India. Whatever I know about him, if he says he makes it happen and if he comes back in Tennis in any form, it'll be great not only for the sport but for the country as well".

Before I wind up, something happened recently which I would share with you. Few days back I met one of Aushim's old acquaintances, Mr. Jitender Gulati who is the owner of Priya Videos and who has video rights of the film 'Shirdi Sai Baba'. Mr. Gulati was susceptible about Aushim and Baba's connect and that reflects what most of his other friends think about him. He very simply asked me, 'Madamji, tell me one thing. I had met Aushim in 2002 when he was doing very well. He was at the top. He had money, bungalows, cars, reputation, companies, fame and was one of the elites. But in these ten years, I have only seen him going down, in fact in these ten years, every time I meet him, I realized that his financial condition was deteriorating. If you say he is doing God's work, tell me why then so much penury and down fall?'

This question made me really think: that's true! If we are on the path of truth and spirituality, our path should be rid of all the obstacles, because, if being on the path of truth brings unhappiness and sadness, how can it be different from the usual path of materialistic growth? A question that I think we need to ask ourselves and the Universe.

One explanation can be that once we have chosen the path, we need to change our style of working, the way Neil Walsh, Famous spiritual writer says 'When everything changes, change everything.'

Aushim has never believed that being on the path of spirituality or healing, one cannot be a businessman or have comfortable, luxurious life and I totally agree with him. But what may be needed is that ways of doing business or living life or dealing with people needs to be changed. As I write these lines, indecision creeps in my mind. Therefore, I decided to wait for the answers like many of you.

On 1st February 2013 when I am penning the last few lines of this book, so much is still happening. Before I stop I want to share why it took so long to create and craft this book. First, it wasn't easy to understand the complexity of the life Aushim has led. Second, it wasn't easy to take out his life from the mercurial being Aushim; and the third and most important, I am not a writer but still something has come up which is a miracle in itself.

As I am writing these last lines, this unpredictable enigma known as Aushim Khetarpal and his even more complicated, unpredictable life has taken another turn.

After ten years of poverty and drudgery, it is being heard that his two listed companies are opening with no penalty or fine (meaning, he gets a clearance from the Government). He has just signed an 11-crore endorsement deal with a natural product company and Sai Dham finally is getting a collaborator.

Great! But we can't wait for more drama to unfold. These deals might go through or may fall back. Aushim is no more concerned because this time he has finally done the biggest and permanent deal of his life which will never fall down because

THE DEAL IS WITH THE DIVINE.